Teaching Gifted and Talented Pupils in the Primary School

Teaching Gifted and Talented Pupils in the Primary School

A Practical Guide

Chris Smith

P·C·P

Paul Chapman
Publishing

First published 2005
Reprinted 2006

 Paul Chapman Publishing
A SAGE Publications Company
1 Oliver's Yard
55 City Road
London EC1Y 1SP

SAGE Publications Inc
2455 Teller Road
Thousand Oaks, California 91320

SAGE Publications India Pvt Ltd
B-42, Panchsheel Enclave
Post Box 4109
New Delhi 110 017

Library of Congress Control Number: 2005921838

A catalogue record for this book is available from the British Library

ISBN-10 1-4129-0318-1   **ISBN-13 978-1-4129-0318-9**
ISBN-10 1-4129-0319-X (pbk)   **ISBN-13 978-1-4129-0319- 6 (pbk)**

Typeset by Pantek Arts Ltd, Maidstone, Kent
Printed in Great Britain by Cromwell Press Ltd, Trowbridge, Wiltshire

Dedication

To my husband Neil who has displayed more patience with me than I deserve and to my mother, Mary H. MacIntyre, who has the highest EQ of anyone I know.

Contents

Tables and Diagrams

About the Author

Over her 21 year career Chris Smith has taught in the primary, secondary and higher sectors of education in Scotland. For most of that time she has been involved in supporting pupils with additional support needs. For the past 15 years this has included the support of gifted and talented pupils. She is currently employed as a lecturer in the Department of Education Studies in the University of Glasgow.

Acknowledgements

There are always people to thank for ideas and input and this book is no exception.

To the SNAP associate tutors, in particular June Orr and Fiona Lyon for reading an early draft of this work, thank you.

To those I have taught beside for allowing me to shamelessly pinch their ideas, in particular John McClosky and Anne Maley, thank you.

To Lorraine Muir for allowing me loose on her class to try out ideas and to her primary six class for their enthusiasm and tolerance, thank you.

To colleagues in the University of Glasgow for their friendship and support, and to Margaret Sutherland and Rae Galbraith in particular for all their feedback and help with the draft chapters, thank you.

Preface

This book is based on a few basic realities.

1   Most gifted and talented children are educated in their local primary school.

2   As a primary teacher you will have children in your class capable of gifted and/or talented behaviours.

3   One of the most difficult aspects of being a primary teacher is providing appropriately for an ever-increasing range of abilities in the class.

By looking closely at how to provide appropriate challenges for gifted and talented pupils we can learn a lot about how to design better activities for all children. This book is about designing activities that encourage all children, and most especially the gifted and talented, to both demonstrate and develop their abilities.

Many writers and researchers[i] have suggested that what teachers and pupils believe about gifts and talents permeate and influence everything that happens in the classroom. These beliefs impact on the ethos that teachers create, the types of activities that they design and offer, and the type of feedback that they give to pupils about their work and about their behaviour. As a result Chapter 1 will look quite closely at this idea of beliefs and their influence on teacher–pupil relationships and pupil performance.

For a long time in education we have tended to concentrate on the differences between pupils[ii]. These differences have been diagnosed and documented with the idea that different treatments are required. This has led to some children being separated off from the mainstream and some teachers believing that special expertise is required in order to teach these different 'types' of children. While recognising that difference and diversity is important we mustn't lose sight of the fact that learners also have an awful lot in common. In primary schools, when we are likely to be teaching mixed ability classes, it is useful to use these 'commonalities' to help us to design activities that include all learners in the class. Chapter 2 will look specifically at what learners have in common.

Following the look at beliefs and commonalities we will spend the rest of the book looking at ways of organising and structuring activities in the primary classroom that provide a sense of community and coherence to what might appear to be a very disparate group of learners. We will concentrate specifically on making sure that high levels of challenge are provided for those children who are ready for it.

Chapter 1

Gifted Children in the Primary Classroom

In this chapter we will:

- Help you think about how your own beliefs about what giftedness is can influence pupil performance.

- Offer a circular model to consider giftedness in the primary classroom.

What teachers and pupils believe about gifts and talents

In primary school we have a huge advantage over our secondary colleagues. We see the children every day for whole days at a time. We, therefore, have ample opportunity to build important, long lasting and robust relationships with our pupils. Every primary school teacher recognises that this is vital, not only to create a positive and pleasant working environment, but because it makes a huge impact on how well pupils perform in our class.

The way that we build these relationships is affected by what we believe a 'good' pupil to be. The way that we build relationships, the way that we talk to pupils and the expectations that we have of individuals are deeply affected by how we believe the human mind works[i]. Research[ii] suggests that what we believe about how the human mind works is often built on unquestioned assumptions.

Implicit theories…reside in the minds of individuals, whether as definitions or otherwise. Such theories need to be discovered rather than invented because they already exist, in some form, in people's heads.[iii]

Forming these implicit theories, while often done unconsciously, is essential because they help us to function effectively in life. The way that they help us is by guiding the way we behave; both what we say and what we do. It is not just teachers, however, who hold implicit beliefs. Children in our classes will hold these beliefs too. They are formed as a result of the way that parents and teachers talk to them and give them feedback about their behaviours and achievements.

In the primary classroom, beliefs are particularly important. Pupils are still forming their beliefs and the primary teacher can have a huge influence on how these develop. They are important to think about because what individuals believe about their own and others' abilities:

- can account for differences in achievement between pupils and by individual pupils over time;

- make a difference to the amount of effort a learner might put into an activity;

- can help to explain depressive reactions by pupils (yes, even in the primary school), to bad experiences in learning;

- and can be used to judge and label both ourselves and others.

There are two very different implicit theories of intelligence[iv].

1   Intelligence is fixed.

2   Intelligence is changeable.

What does believing that intelligence is fixed mean for pupils?

If pupils believe intelligence is fixed it means that they are likely to believe that they were born either clever or stupid and that they will stay that way for the rest of their lives. They also tend to believe that school success and school tests are a good indicator of who is clever and who is not. As a result of this they will predict their future success on the basis of today's performance. They will offer reasons for success and failure that are related to personal adequacy or inadequacy. For example, failure may be accounted for by poor memory or low intelligence (I just can't do maths!). Likewise success is because they have a natural aptitude for such things or because their parents were good at them. Such pupils are more likely to show aversion to tasks that they do badly in by saying they are bored or through feelings of anxiety.

Believing intelligence is fixed means that undertaking activities is about performance. Pupils with this belief might worry about how much ability they have or don't have to complete a task. They calculate this by comparing themselves with others. These pupils are more likely to be competitive and can become driven with the need to show that they are the cleverest in the class. They may develop a tendency to choose the easy option and avoid harder tasks that might show them up to be less 'clever' than they thought they were (or that they would want others to perceive them to be). They believe that being clever means that all tasks and activities should be completed very easily therefore having to work hard at something indicates that they are not very clever. Only success that comes easily is valued because this is what indicates high ability.

Questions to consider

- Can I recognise any pupils who might have a fixed view of intelligence?

- To what extent do I have a fixed view of intelligence of my own learning?

What does believing that intelligence is changeable mean for pupils?

If a pupil believes that intelligence is changeable it means that they are likely to believe that how intelligent they can become is in their own hands. If they work hard they can become better at things and this improvement is an indicator of their intelligence. They rely less on test scores to give them a measure of their abilities and do not believe that test scores and school success will predict their future success or failure. Believing that intelligence is changeable means that failure is more likely to be put down to environmental or temporary contributors such as choosing the wrong topics to study. Equally success is generally attributed to sheer hard work.

Believing in changeable intelligence means that undertaking activities is about mastery. Pupils with this belief strive for personal improvement and so tend to be less competitive. They compete with themselves rather than other people. These pupils may develop a tendency to choose challenging work, rather than easy work, because that means they will learn more. Getting things wrong – within reason – does not bother them because failure is perceived as part of the learning process. These pupils have a belief that if you work hard you can become more able. Trying something really hard and achieving even only part of it shows you that you have improved and have learned new abilities that you did not have before. These pupils are more likely to be able to identify some things that they good at and some things that they are not so good at, believing that people are different and there are lots of ways of being able. These pupils seek to try lots of things because the experience of trying is enjoyable.

Teachers sometimes assume that gifted and talented pupils hold a belief that intelligence is changeable. They can be identified because of characteristics such as willingness to choose hard activities, and willingness to work hard. In fact some gifted and/or talented pupils believe strongly that intelligence is fixed. They will avoid hard work, try to do things with the minimum effort, and can be highly competitive. In this way the idea of implicit theories might help us to understand some aspects of underachievement, disaffection and disengagement.

I have presented here characteristics of the extreme positions that implicit theories can create and these two positions mean very different things for individuals (see Table 1.1). You may have started to recognise a few pupils. We need to be

Table 1.1 *Comparison of pupils' implicit theories*

Questions pupils try to answer	Fixed theory answer	Changeable theory answer
Why am I the way I am?	I was born clever. I am this way because my mum and/or dad is clever.	I work hard to be good at things. I am this way because my mum and/or dad encourage me. Certain things interest me more than others. I get the chance to try different things.
How do I assess my own intelligence?	People tell me I am clever. My results in tests and in class tell me how clever I am. Being first in the class means I am the cleverest in the class. Doing badly in a test tells me I am not as clever as I thought. How easy or hard I find things tell me how clever I am.	How much I improve tells me how clever I am. If I work hard and do well it tells me I am clever. People tell me that I am working hard and am doing well. I can see that I am better today at things than I was the last time I did them.
What does this tell me?	I will always be clever. I am clever at lots of things. I should get things right first time, most of the time. I should always get good results. I should always do better than those who are less clever than me.	The harder I work the better I will do. I might not be clever at everything. I might just be clever at a small number of things. The things I am clever at might not be in school. I might make lots of mistakes but this helps me learn more. I shouldn't worry too much about whom I am better or worse than.
How might this make me act?	I will avoid failure at all costs. I might panic if I start to find something hard. I may cheat rather than fail. I don't like to ask for help because that would be an admission of failure.	I like to try hard things and learn from trying. If I am faced with a really hard problem I will seek out help from others. I need to work hard to make sure that I do well.
Type of learner	Fragile. Sees learning as a competition.	Robust. Sees learning as a personal journey.

careful, however. We don't want to start labelling pupils as one type of theorist or another; labelling has not helped us in the past. Rather let us be aware that believing certain things can impact on how pupils learn in our classrooms and that as teachers we have the power to support or change their implicit theories. Whether we support or change implicit theories of intelligence in a positive way, however, will depend on the theory that we ourselves hold.

Questions to consider

- Can I recognise any pupils who might believe that intelligence is changeable?

- To what extent do I believe that my own intelligence is changeable?

It can be useful to find out a little more about what the pupils in your class believe. Asking pupils the questions on the sheet on page 6 will provide you with some more information.

Think about your own beliefs by considering the questionnaire on page 7.

The more that you have agreed with the statements in the questionnaire on what you believe, the more you are likely to believe that intelligence is fixed. The more you have disagreed with the statements in the questionnaire, the more likely it is that you believe intelligence is changeable. What might this mean for how we teach? The examples below describe the extremes of holding one view or another. Most teachers are – quite rightly – somewhere between the two.

What does believing that intelligence is fixed mean for teachers?

Teachers who believe strongly that intelligence is fixed are likely to believe that some pupils have more innate ability than others. It is the teacher's job to bring out the best in the children; in other words, help them to make the best of what they were born with. These teachers believe that the best way to provide for gifted and talented pupils is to identify which pupils were born with particular gifts and talents and to educate them accordingly. Although they do not believe education can make children more intelligent and that each child has a limit, they do believe that all children can improve their performance.

What am I good at?

1 In school I am good at _____

_____

2 Outside school I am good at _____

_____

3 I am good at these things because _____

_____

4 In school I am not so good at _____

_____

5 Outside school I am not so good at _____

_____

6 I am not good at these things because _____

_____

7 Do you think you could become good at these things? If yes, how? ____

_____

8 Is there anything that you think you will never be able to do well? If yes, why is this?

_____

9 What is more important – to be the best in the class or do better than you did last week? _____

_____

What do you believe?

Try answering the following questions.

What do I believe?

1   Gifted individuals form a group that can be identified early in their school career and remains the same over time.

Agree   Disagree

2   Gifted individuals are born with high intelligence.

Agree   Disagree

3   Gifted and talented children need different forms of teaching and support from other children.

Agree   Disagree

4   Because of their differences gifted children need to be educated separately from other children.

Agree   Disagree

5   Teachers need special training and skills to teach gifted children.

Agree   Disagree

6   Giftedness is genetic and cannot be changed.

Agree   Disagree

7   Gifted and talented children need competition to keep them on their toes.

Agree   Disagree

Belief in fixed intelligence means that intelligence is viewed more as a singular concept, as a general energy (often referred to as 'g') that flows into all that we do. If pupils are intelligent then they are likely to be good at a range of things rather than one very specific area. It is believed that pupils with high intelligence can focus their mental energy (g) towards almost any aspect of school life.

Teachers with this view might be more likely to support the organisation of pupils in or across classes into top, middle and bottom sets or groups. The composition of sets will be viewed as stable because such arrangements reflect the natural order of things in the classroom. Most work required of pupils will be individual in nature and collaborative work will be seen as a way in which 'better' pupils can help out with 'poorer' pupils. Success in school and beyond can be predicted accurately and early in a pupil's school career. In essence this view ascribes to the genetic origins of intelligence as fixed, singular (g), located almost exclusively within the pupil and possible to measure or identify through standardised tests (possibly IQ) and school exams.

A belief in the fixed and general nature of intelligence will support fairly tight frameworks of assessment within schools. Examinations and national testing are seen as good indicators of pupils' abilities. Such teachers might be interested in identifying the strengths and weaknesses that lie within pupils as this is where intelligence resides. They might be less convinced about ongoing classroom assessment because the performance from such assessment may be affected by factors that lie outwith the pupil such as help from parents, other pupils etc.

Teachers who believe in the fixed nature of intelligence tend to encourage performance goals in the classroom. In other words getting things right and performing well is important: mistakes are discouraged and are seen as evidence of a drop in standards. Activities and expectations are tailored to what is perceived to be an individual pupil's intelligence level. Pupils are compared one to another and competition is encouraged within and beyond the classroom as a means of motivating pupils and extending performance. Good work is recognised, valued and celebrated as something for others to emulate.

Believing in fixed intelligence focuses teacher comment and description on the pupils themselves, for example 'you're really good at that'; 'she's very clever'; 'you are a very good boy'. It is also reflected in teachers' expectations of what pupils can achieve. Believing that intelligence is fixed and innate will lead to high expectations of those identified as being born with high intelligence.

What does believing that intelligence is changeable mean for teachers?

Teachers who believe that intelligence is changeable tend to believe that the environment is the most important influence on how intelligent an individual becomes. This means that the teacher's role is to help his or her pupils to become more intelligent through the classroom environment. Whether pupils do or do not demonstrate their intelligences depends on whether or not they are given the appropriate opportunities and encouragement. Every child in the class is a possible gifted pupil.

Because intelligence is determined by the environment it is not possible to group or set pupils by ability successfully since setting and/or grouping can limit opportunities for some pupils. In addition setting, for these teachers, implies that schools can identify capacity within a pupil through school success. For teachers who believe that intelligence is changeable there are no genetic limits or capacities to an individual's intelligences therefore it is not possible to predict success or failure beyond school for any pupil. If circumstances change then much more may become possible for an individual. Conversely, a change of circumstance may limit an individual's progress. All pupils can be gifted and/or talented if they are provided with the right environment and opportunities.

Intelligence is not a singular concept indicating a general energy but much more about separate and distinct areas of ability. Limits cannot be assumed or predicted for individuals nor can intelligences be tested or examined. The role of education is to help all pupils develop and increase their intelligences. This theory is epitomised by the famous quote from Watson[v]:

> ...*give me a dozen healthy infants, well-formed, and my own specified world to bring them up and I'll guarantee to take any one at random and train him to become any type of specialist I might select – doctor, lawyer, artist, merchant-chief and, yes, even beggar-man thief, regardless of his talents, penchants, tendencies, abilities, vocations, and race of his ancestors...*

Teachers who believe in changeable intelligence are likely to prefer classroom assessment rather than examinations and standardised tests as a good indicator of pupils' progress and demonstration of abilities. These teachers will attempt to gather a wide range of assessment evidence that accounts for factors that lie in the environment. The information will be gathered from a wide range of sources and cover a wide range of behaviours.

Teachers who believe in changeable intelligence encourage mastery goals in the classroom. In other words working through a problem is more important than getting a correct answer: mistakes are positively encouraged and are seen as an indicator of the learning process in action. Pupils are encouraged to track their own progress over time and not to compare themselves with others.

Good work is recognised, valued and celebrated but not as an example for others to emulate since everyone has to find their own way of doing things. Feedback and description of pupils will focus on their behaviour or their work, for example, 'I particularly liked the style in which you wrote that piece'; 'did you think that was your best piece of work?'; 'this is a really hard problem to solve but you managed to complete three sections.' Collaborative work is encouraged as this is seen as a way in which pupils can learn from one another. Groups can achieve more than individuals working on their own and all individuals in the group benefit from the collaboration.

Table 1.2 *Comparison of teachers' implicit theories*

Questions teachers try to answer	Fixed theory answer	Changeable theory answer
Why are pupils different from one another?	Intelligence is genetic. Some children are born with more intelligence than others.	Different life chances mean that there are vast differences between pupils' attainment.
How do I sort out who is able to do what?	Intelligence can be identified through a fairly short list of key abilities. If pupils demonstrate these abilities then they can be identified as gifted and/or talented. School work and standardised tests are a good way of sorting out who is most intelligent. Tests of different kinds help to identify capacity in pupils. They can be used to predict who will do well and who will not.	I have to profile pupils across a whole range of intelligent behaviours. I have to provide opportunities for pupils to demonstrate all the behaviours that I would consider an indicator of developed intelligences. I cannot predict who will succeed and who will not on the basis of present performance. I can only offer next steps.
What does this tell me?	I cannot make pupils more intelligent, I can only help draw out what they already have. I can identify who has most and who has least intelligence in my class and then organise them on that basis. Competitions and comparisons are good methods for motivating pupils and giving feedback.	I can help make pupils more intelligent. It is not possible to identify a group who might be considered gifted and/or talented. The combination of strengths and development needs for each pupil will help to tell me what the next steps are. Schools alone cannot identify all the intelligent behaviours that pupils might demonstrate so I need to gather information from elsewhere.

How might this make me act?	I support streaming or setting as a way of organising pupils. I celebrate and display the best work of the class. I value individual achievement very highly. I feed back on whether or not the pupil is performing to his or her potential. I can predict who will succeed and who will not. I will identify those pupils in my class who are gifted/talented.	I support mixed ability groups as a way of organising pupils. I value collaborative achievement very highly. I give feedback to pupils on their work and effort in class. I celebrate and display pupils' best efforts.
System of education created	Exclusive. Based on sifting and sorting.	Inclusive. Based on individual needs.

Is it best to foster fixed or changeable beliefs?

Some of the literature suggests that the 'right' implicit theory for teachers to hold is a changeable theory[vi]. This is because teachers who believe that intelligence is changeable are more likely to encourage mastery orientated beliefs in the pupils they teach. It would appear that mastery orientated beliefs seem to encourage a more positive response to learning in pupils.

Mastery orientated beliefs, then, might be most crucial for those pupils who are turned off from school learning. For pupils to identify with the purposes of schooling they need to gain a sense of belonging. A sense of belonging requires the individual to believe that they are important and are, or at least can be, an active participant in the learning process. Mastery orientated goals, where the focus is not on the adequacy of one's ability but on factors within the control of the individual, are more likely to provide the conditions necessary for this self-perception to be attained[vii]. Unlike mastery orientated goals, performance goals are more likely to separate individuals from their peers on the basis of performance in class and decrease their sense of belonging.

However, even for those who might ascribe to the need to encourage mastery orientation there are some myths around about how this should be done.

1   It is often believed that the more pupils experience success in school the more mastery orientated qualities are fostered. However, from research it

would appear that success in itself does little to boost pupils' desire for challenge or their ability to cope with setbacks. In one piece of research[viii] children who believed in a fixed intelligence theory, even after a string of successes, assigned their one and only failure to a lack of intelligence. They lost faith in their intellect to the extent that they believed that they could not even repeat prior successes.

2   It is believed that praise encourages mastery orientated qualities but we have to be careful with praise. It can matter a great deal: who gives it; when it is given; why it is given and for what it is given. We can cause 'damage' with empty praise[ix].

3   Confidence is a key to mastery orientated qualities. Many so called 'confident' individuals have actually very fragile confidence in their abilities. Their confidence is quickly shaken and they do not wish their intelligence too stringently tested. Such pupils will avoid work that they find difficult and in which they may not perform well.

4   Gifted and talented pupils are mastery orientated: this is untrue. Some gifted and/or talented pupils hold strong fixed intelligence theories and are heavily orientated towards performance goals.

The thing to remember is that a bit of both (mastery and performance) might be the best thing. If we think of Olympic gold medallists like Ian Thorpe (swimmer) or Matthew Pinsent (rower) then it would be best for them to have mastery goals for their training sessions (where they try to improve on their own past performances and pay close attention to their own progress over time) and have performance goals for competitions (where the number one goal is to compare themselves to others with the goals of being first and the best). The questions for teachers are three-fold.

- To what extent do I subscribe to a fixed theory or a changeable theory of intelligence?

- Is this having any impact on pupils in my class?

- Do I think I have the balance right?

But what does this mean for mainstream schools in the meantime? How might schools review their beliefs and practice? Does practice in the school lean towards a particular view of intelligence? Is the range of provision currently available sufficient and suitable? The next section will try to address some of these issues.

A circular model to consider gifts and talents

This model[x] (Diagram 1.1) is based on the idea of identification through provision[xi] and the ways that teachers and pupils interact with one another in the classroom[xii]. It offers a holistic approach to the identification of gifted and talented pupils. The circular process ensures that the identification of abilities is ongoing rather than a one-off test or activity.

The model has four steps.

Diagram 1.1   **The circular model of identification**

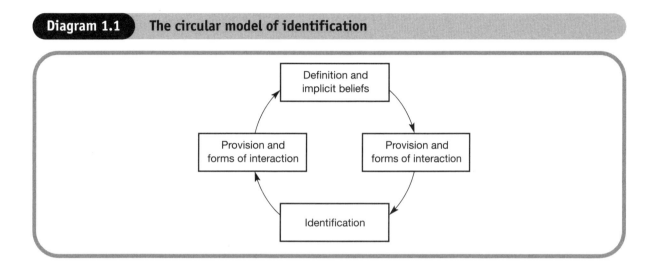

Step one: What do I believe about gifted and talented children?

You have begun step one by reading through and thinking about the questions posed in the first part of this chapter. What teachers believe can have a huge impact on whether pupils demonstrate abilities or not. These beliefs help to create particular cultures in schools and classrooms. Some cultures are more helpful in facilitating achievement and motivation than others. There are particular difficulties for gifted and talented pupils if the culture that determines provision rests on the idea that intelligence is fixed, biologically determined and is located wholly within the individual. Such beliefs generate a concentration on performance goals in the classroom that is evidenced by social comparisons and normative evaluations.

Rather than compare one pupil with another it may be more helpful to identify the sorts of behaviours that teachers believe a gifted and/or talented individual should be able demonstrate in the different curricular areas. General lists of intelligent behaviours to be encouraged in all pupils exist. One is provided below[xiii].

- Being open minded and flexible about ideas and solutions.

- Being aware of your own and others' thinking, behaviours and feelings.

- Being able to work with others collaboratively.

- Being accurate and seeking accuracy.

- Being able to monitor and control your behaviour, learning and work.

- Being able to plan appropriately.

- Being able to respond appropriately to feedback.

- Being able to identify and use necessary resources.

There may also be some specific intelligent behaviours that can only be identified when pupils are undertaking particular activities. Such lists, however, should not be seen as a checklist with pupils being identified as being gifted and talented on the basis of a set number of ticks. Rather, it provides a tool to examine the curriculum. This allows us to ensure that the opportunities exist for pupils to demonstrate, develop and learn how to behave in these ways.

There are some key questions that should be considered in step one.

- What definitions of intelligence exist?

- Do I agree with any of these? If not what would my definition be?

- Do I hold a particular implicit theory of intelligence? What does this mean for pupils in my class?

- Do pupils in my class hold a particular implicit theory of intelligence? Is this impacting on their learning in any way?

- Do I identify pupils or sets of behaviour and what criteria do I use?

- Are some criteria specific to particular curricular areas or are they all general?

Step two: What provision currently exists and how do I relate to pupils in my class?

Once some discussion has taken place about what intelligence is and what might be looked for the next step involves an audit of the curricular provision currently available and the pedagogy currently in place. If provision is dominated by a narrow range of opportunities and limited challenge then it will be impossible for pupils to demonstrate or develop anything other than a small range of intelligent behaviours. Opportunities must exist for intelligent behaviours, not only to be demonstrated but to be developed and taught. If gaps exist in the present provision then they require to be filled.

Once the curriculum has been audited for opportunities that match our definitions and understanding of what the full range of intelligent behaviours might be, the next step is to examine our own practices as teachers. The ways in which we interact with pupils (how we phrase feedback, how we support and encourage), the messages we give them (both implicit and explicit) and the media we choose to give deliver messages (written, verbal, and non verbal), in other words the culture we create in our classrooms, all have an impact on whether or not pupils will be able or feel able to demonstrate intelligent behaviours. It may be that a range of opportunities exist but if the culture in the class is dominated by performance goals then some children may feel unable to demonstrate intelligent behaviours that they have already mastered. In fact they may be more comfortable demonstrating these intelligent behaviours elsewhere, for example it takes the demonstration of many intelligent behaviours to plan a robbery and work collaboratively to carry it out successfully.

Some questions that might be posed during step two.

- Do I have high expectations of all pupils in my class?

- Do I provide a full range of opportunities for pupils to demonstrate intelligent behaviours?

- Do I teach the skills necessary for these behaviours to develop in those who are not yet demonstrating them?

- How do I feed back on success and failure?

- Is it safe to fail in my class?

- Is it safe to demonstate intelligent behaviours in my class?

Step three: Who is coping well with the most challenging activities and who might need extra challenge?

Once the opportunities for the demonstration of intelligent behaviours have been identified and put into place the assessment process begins. This process is about recording where and when it is that pupils demonstrate the behaviours that teachers would wish to encourage in all pupils. It is also about asking for help from others to identify where and when a pupil demonstrates them. The pupils themselves should be involved. In this way school starts to reach out into the community and into the pupils' lives for evidence that abilities are beginning to form or have already formed. There are three things to be on the lookout for.

1   The regular and sustained demonstration of intelligent behaviours by individuals.

2   The occasional and sporadic demonstration of these intelligent behaviours by individuals

3   The demonstration of these intelligent behaviours by individuals in contexts other than school.

Step four: What additional provision can I put in place?

From stage three there will be a range of opportunities identified as being possibilities for pupils to demonstrate and learn intelligent behaviours. Pupils will be demonstrating these to varying degrees of sophistication and regularity. There will also be a range of contexts identified where certain individuals can demonstrate intelligent behaviours outwith the confines of the school. It is about designing progress and coherence in challenge so that there are always further challenging opportunities available.

It is necessary to go back to provision and make sure that, for those who are demonstrating such behaviours in a regular and sustained way, there are activities and opportunities to extend their already developed abilities. For those demonstrating sporadically it is about searching for opportunities to help develop these so that they become more sustained and regular.

Stage three will also have provided essential information about pupils who might be demonstrating intelligent behaviours outside of school in other contexts. An analysis of where and when this is occurring might help to identify what it is that the school or teacher can do to help transfer these behaviours into learning based activities in the classroom.

Some questions that might be considered in step four

- Are these the pupils I would have expected to be identified?

- Might there be pupils not currently demonstrating abilities who could if the activities or culture changed in the class?

- For those who are already able to demonstate their abilities in particular areas to a high degree (either before or after tuition) are there sufficiently challenging activities and experiences which allow them to develop their abilities further?

Back to step one: What do I believe about gifted and talented children now?

It is time to revisit out original thoughts about what intelligence means and what it is that we are trying to do.

- Are there new theories or research to think about?

- Does the definition of intelligence require change or amendment?

- How is my theory of intelligence impacting on my class?

- Have I been able to identify pupils in my class with particular views of intelligence?

- Do I need to revisit the criteria I use when assessing intelligent behaviours?

- Does my list of intelligent behaviours require change or amendment?

- Am I collecting information from a wide enough range of contexts?

Conclusion

Points for reflection:

- How much do you think that the beliefs we hold about intelligence make a difference to pupils' achievements and performance?

- To what extent is the model of giftedness in operation in your school linear or cyclical?

- Does the system of identification in your school rest on the performance of individuals or on the provision made available?

Chapter 2

Principles of Good Practice for All Learners

In this chapter we will look at:

- A framework of support for teachers and children.

- Elements of a good learning experience.

- The importance of culture as a context for challenging activities.

- A step by step guide to designing activities.

A framework of support for teachers and children

If inclusionary classrooms are committed to serving all students they must choose to include, both physically and philosophically, even the more extremely gifted children as well as children with the most severe disabilities. This means more for both groups than simply being in attendance in the regular classroom, it means respecting and teaching one's students to respect the unique developmental paths of each individual, no matter how unusual; providing access to a developmentally appropriate curriculum; and providing related support services.[i]

The greatest concerns about educational provision for gifted and talented pupils has related to the coherence and progression of learning. A large amount of provision is inappropriate.[ii]

We provide a pullout programme, an accelerated course, an honours class, a special class or some other program with a clever acronym and consider that we have provided adequately for the gifted.[iii]

A lot of provision is *ad hoc*:

... fragmentary learning experiences, lacking in complex form, long-range purpose, or clear directionality.[iv]

Providing an appropriate, coherent and planned programme for upwards of 30 pupils in a class can be a daunting task and we cannot be expected to do it on our own.

There are several layers to the education system: national education departments, local education authorities, schools and classrooms. The education system is also part of a wider range of community services. As teachers we need to be able to draw on an appropriate range of these layers and services if we are to be able to provide appropriately for all the pupils in our class (Table 2.1).

Table 2.1 *A framework of support for gifted and talented pupils*

Layer of support	Provision
Classroom	A positive ethos built on good relationships High expectations of all children Choice and variety of activities A range of levels and challenge within community activities Enhancement and enrichment of the curriculum Curriculum compaction and substitute activities Individual Education Programmes A range and variety of within class grouping
School	Within stage or cross stage groupings G&T coordinator/pupil support services Special, short term, pull-out programmes Visits/guest speakers Specialist provision (eg music tuition) Out of school enrichment activities Decisions about accleration for individuals
Local authority	Cross school groupings Online links between schools and individuals Mentoring Computer links Specialist support (in Scotland SNAP associate tutors) Out of school enrichment activities and courses Coordinated Support Plan (Scotland)
National	Policy and legislation National advisory body (in Scotland, SNAP) National Academy for G&T Youth (England) National Grid for Learning website – advice for teachers Online courses for individuals and groups

Table 2.1 suggests that, if teachers are to be able to provide a coherent and planned curriculum for individual pupils, we need to be supported at various levels. Too often the responsibility has been left to classroom teachers. Ideas and reforms cascade down for teachers to implement and the result is a burden too heavy to bear. Rather than feel all the responsibility falls to them, class teachers should be able to draw on a variety of different provisions targeted to support their work with individual pupils.

The ideal, then, is to have layers of support that permeate all levels of the education system. The foundation of it all, however, is what happens in the primary classroom and how we design and provide for a range of levels of challenge within community activities. Instead of concentrating on how the children differ from one another let us think about what sorts of experiences make up good learning experiences for all children and then design all activities with these principles at their heart.

Elements of a good learning experience

There are four interactive elements of learning[v] (see Diagram 2.1) that can apply to all learners and will encourage more meaningful engagement with learning in the classroom. The four elements are agency, reflection, collaboration and culture.

| Diagram 2.1 | The interactive elements of learning |

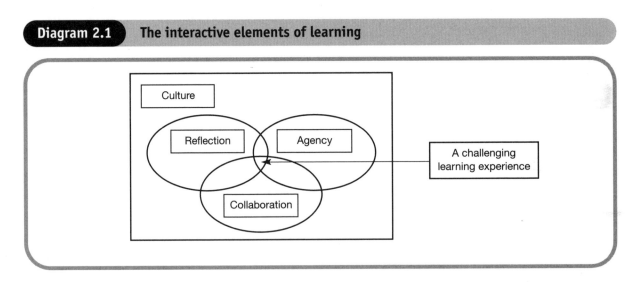

Activities identified as offering appropriate challenge for able pupils share certain characteristics. They provide opportunities for agency, reflection and collaboration within a supportive and challenging culture. Different activities will lend themselves to one of the elements more than others and so the emphasis may change from activity to activity.

Agency

Agency is about control. How much are the learners in control of what and how they learn? Are they active participants in the learning process – do they have ownership of it? Because the learners have had a part to play in what it is that has to be learned they will have a much greater degree of understanding and of knowledge which is much more likely to be retained. In short, agency means that the aims for learning are negotiated and shared with the learner. When designing activities this will involve:

- negotiating tasks;

- offering choice;

- encouraging children to plan and map out their own learning pathways (this way they have an idea of the big picture and where they are going);

- and agreeing aims for learning at class, group and individual level.

Reflection

Reflection is about the learner understanding for him or herself what it is and how it is that they have learned something. This process is called metacognition: it is the ability to understand your own learning and make links to other areas of knowledge and understanding. Transferring knowledge and understanding can be helped by paying attention to the opportunities pupils have for reflection in the learning process: What did I learn today? How did I learn that? Why could I manage to do this particular problem here in maths but not in geography? Is there anything I learned today which I can use in other subject areas? Encouraging reflection will mean that:

- thinking time is built into the activity;

- links across the curriculum are made explicit (cross curricular or themed projects can be excellent for this);

- discussion times are available for small groups as well as the whole class;

- reflective activities feed into the assessment system for the lesson, unit or project.

Collaboration

Collaboration is about working with others in ways that bring together a range of expertise and knowledge so that new and more difficult problems can be solved. Collaboration, unfortunately, can be reduced to groups of pupils seated together doing individual work or groups of children working together to solve a problem. However, they often share the same knowledge and understanding rather than being able to contribute a range of knowledge and expertise. True collaboration, as opposed to cooperation or parallel working, involves learners interacting with one another and contributing a variety of expertise and knowledge. We need to examine how and why we group children to ensure that true collaboration is achieved. This means that:

- opportunities need to exist for children to work with different groups for different purposes e.g. interest, ability, mixed ability, friendship, age and stage related, cross age and stage etc.

Culture

Culture is about the histories and influences that form our lives – both personal and professional. Culture is a very strong influence on how we behave, what we learn and how we apply what we learn to a variety of situations. We are all part of a range of cultures. There is a British culture but equally those from ethnic minorities may also experience their culture of origin. Schools can have a general culture but also have sub-cultures. One school may have, for example, a culture of academic success and exam excellence but also have a sub-culture of boys underachieving. Culture is easy to experience, it is harder to describe and almost impossible to define but its importance cannot be underestimated. We shall spend the next section thinking about the culture that we create in our classroom before turning to the steps involved in designing activities that account for the other three interactive elements of learning.

The importance of culture as a context for challenging activities

Creating the right culture, where the abilities of all children can develop and thrive, depends fundamentally on the relationships between the people in the class. Relationships are about creating positive and encouraging relationships between the teacher and the pupils as well as between pupils. All teachers strive for a positive and affirming climate in their class but this is sometimes seen as luck rather than design. If we were to consciously consider the elements that contribute to positive relationships in a classroom then we would do well to think about the following.

- knowledge;
- sending the right messages;
- security;
- links to the world outside the classroom.

Knowledge

We all try to get to know the children in our classes well and by the end of a year we usually know them very well indeed. The quest is to gather enough information – to provide an all-round picture – to enable us to do our jobs effectively without intruding unnecessarily on the private lives of our pupils. We have to get the balance right because some children feel very vulnerable if they think that others know too much about what they consider to be private or sensitive details about them. Care and delicacy is required. Consider what you would be comfortable sharing with others outside the home – your work colleagues or headteacher for example – and then consider if we sometimes expect children to share details that we ourselves would not.

While we all recognise the importance of getting to know the children, we sometimes do not pay enough attention to their need to know us – not simply as teachers but as people who have lives outside the classroom. I am not suggesting that we start to share intimate details about out private lives but it is sometimes easy to forget that the children need an all-round picture of us just as much as we need an all-round picture of them.

Sending the right messages

Our communication with children is not merely the things we say, although these are vitally important, it is also about other silent messages that are transmitted.

CASE STUDY

One class I observed were studying the Scottish Wars of Independence. Robert clearly knew a great deal about the topic and was keen to let the teacher see this. However, he soon got the message that it was not helpful to the teacher for him to know too much because he was never asked to contribute to the class or to answer a question. In fact this was confirmed in a lesson early on when the teacher said 'You seem to know all this Robert so put your hand down and give the rest a chance'. He spent the next six weeks studying a topic he already knew and understood well. He no doubt learned a valuable lesson in the disadvantages of being ahead of the class.

While children will understand that they cannot always have our one-to-one attention we need to recognise moments when individuals require to be prioritised. Do we favour some children more than others? While we would not mean to do this it is sometimes difficult to know. It becomes unconscious. It is often the case that we are trying to send a very positive message but it is being picked up and interpreted differently by the child.

Some children, because they are good at a good many things, find themselves being overloaded with responsibilities and extra tasks but because they are anxious to please they do not always know how to say no.

CASE STUDY

In one class I taught in as a support teacher Fiona always came to me rather than the class teacher. I suggested to her that she might like to ask the class teacher about a particular problem to which she replied 'I'd rather come to you, Mrs X doesn't like me.' In fact this was not the case. Mrs X liked Fiona a great deal. She felt that because Fiona was ahead of the rest of the class in her work and could work well independently it was best to leave her to get on with her work on her own. From Mrs X's point of view this was a compliment, Fiona was a good worker and could be trusted to work alone. From Fiona's point of view this was rejection by the teacher and she felt she was being ignored because the teacher did not like her.

CASE STUDY

Mark was a good 'all-rounder' in school. He was not only top of his class in school work but was also excellent at drama and sports. As a result Mark was involved in everything, he was editor of the school newspaper, he played on the school football team, he was taking part in the school Christmas show, he was always asked to be one of the team of children that greeted any visitors that the school had and he contributed regularly to the school assemblies. His mother approached the school one day to say that Mark was becoming very moody at home and was not sleeping well. He was reluctant to go to school and she was very worried about him. After some careful investigation it was found that Mark was simply overloaded with requests to represent the school and he did not know how to say 'no'. He also did not know what to say 'no' to. He liked everything individually but altogether it was too much. Although his behaviour in school had remained exemplary his frustrations and anxieties had become apparent at home.

The way that we organise our classroom can also send messages to the children.

CASE STUDY

The school was being inspected. One year 5 class had been put into groups according to their ability in written English. The children were working on sentence construction on the day that the class was to be observed by an inspector. The inspector sat with the green group, next to Julie, as he took notes. Julie became very interested in what the inspector was writing and eventually leaned over and asked 'what are you doing?' The inspector replied that he was taking notes of things that were going on in the class. Julie thought about this for a moment and then asked 'are you putting in capital letters and full stops?' 'Yes I am' replied the inspector. At this point Julie leaned over and whispered 'you're in the wrong group then' you should be over there in the red group.'

I am sure the intention of the class teacher in this story would have been to place children in groups according to their ability so that work at an appropriate level could be provided. There is no merit in asking children to undertake tasks that are too far beyond their current level of ability. However, it was clear to Julie that her group was not expected to use capital letters and full stops.

Expectations are funny things and often really difficult to get right. It is often said that we should have high expectations of all children. I agree but what does this mean? We surely cannot expect more of some children than they are able to provide at that point in time. Having our expectations too high would be as bad as having them too low. I have come to the conclusion that it is really about opportunity and being open to being surprised. Julie clearly felt that she should not do capital letters and full stops; the way the class was set up was preventing her from trying. This is where it is important to make a range of opportunities available to all children. Providing choice from this range will allow them to surprise us.

How we respond to children's choices and attempts is important. Some feedback is more positive than others. To be positive it should be:

- **Honest.** This can be a really tricky. I remember a student coming to me and saying 'I want to be positive Chris, but this work is very poor and needs a lot of work.' We had a long conversation about how we provide feedback that can be both honest and positive. Much of our conversation was about helping the child to make their own judgements about the work.

- **Specific and clear** so that the pupils know exactly what to do to improve the work. One pupil I supported in an after-school club came to me with a story she had written in class. 'The teacher has told me to go away and think about how I can make it better but I don't know how.' Vague feedback is worse than no feedback at all.

- **Private rather than public and avoid comparison with others.** It can prove embarrassing to have one's successes or indeed failures made public. The worst, of course, is when the feedback is both public and a comparison. I remember vividly when I myself was at school one poor girl in the class constantly being compared to her sister who was two years above. More recently I was in a class where the teacher remarked to Shakil that he should try to be more like Darren. My heart went out to both of them. Both had just been put in an impossible situation. Some public recognition for significant achievements can be very helpful and motivate children to further achievements but these should be carefully managed according to individual preferences.

- **Related to work or behaviour rather than the person.** Rather than comment that David is a 'really nice boy' it is more positive and helpful to offer examples of behaviour, such as 'David did a really nice thing the other day, he helped Sally in the playground after she fell.' Rather than comment that

Andrew is 'very clever' it is much more helpful to identify what he has achieved, such as 'Andrew did three problems yesterday in maths that were really difficult and he got all of them correct.'

Much of what we know about feedback relates back to what we know about the individuals in our class. Knowing that Ahmed will work at his best and produce incredible results when we push him and give him tight timelines within which to work is important. However, we also need to know that he will become distressed if he is given too many things to do at once. While Ahmed can cope with being pushed hard, Katie needs more subtle and gentle encouragement.

Messages are sent through what we say and what we do. However, more than just what we say and do it is about what we feel. Nurturing a positive culture in the class involves acknowledging emotions: our own and those of the children. We can all have off days. We all have things going on in our lives that impact on how we feel on a day-to-day basis. It is not always possible to leave these emotions at the front door as we head for school in the morning. One teacher I worked with used emotion cards. Everyone in the class, the teacher included, would choose an emotion card first thing in the morning to illustrate how they were feeling. The cards could be changed as moods changed throughout the day. The cards helped the teacher notice that emotions can be contagious. If she was in a good mood and feeling energetic and enthusiastic about the day, the pupils tended to feel much more positive as the day went on. She also found that knowing many of her class were feeling good helped her when she was in a less positive mood herself. If they were all pretty down at the beginning of a day then they could work together to try to change the mood of the class.

The only way of keeping on top of how the messages we send are being received is to encourage honest feedback from the children. Listening to children and hearing their interpretation of what happens in class is the only way we can be sure that our intentions are in line with the results.

Security

From brain research we know that children who are distressed find it impossible to learn in the classroom. I am specifically using the word distress because we can be pushed to work at our limits when we are stressed to a certain degree. I felt quite stressed by having a tight deadline to complete this book, but it was also a very motivating factor. A certain amount of pressure and a certain amount of stress can in fact be good things to make us perform at our best. The problem occurs when this moves from acceptable levels of stress to distress. The point at which this happens is different for us all and what causes distress can be very different from person to person. Creating a culture, therefore, that accounts for the very different ways in which we are affected by stress and distress is one of the most difficult aspects of teaching. There are five things that we might want to think about when we consider security (both physical and mental) in the classroom.

1 **Confidence.**
   a. Are the children confident that they will never be ridiculed or embarrassed?
   b. Do they feel it is safe to take risks with their learning?
   c. Do they feel secure enough to try new things and perhaps get them wrong or do badly?

2 **Consistency.**
   a. Are your expectations and feedback consistent, that is, it will not change from day to day or week to week?

3 **Fairness.**
   a. Do the children feel that they are treated fairly, that others are not favoured or that they are not favoured over others?
   b. Do they feel that feedback is honest, accurate and helpful in taking forward their learning?

4 **Clear boundaries.**
   a. Do children know exactly what the accepted behaviours are in the class?
   b. Were they party to drawing up the class rules?

5 **Physical safety.**
   a. Are relationships in the class such that children are helpful and positive towards one another?
   b. Are any pupils in fear of their physical safety in the playground, outside school or at home?

Links to the world outside the classroom

Is the culture of the classroom consistent with or contradictory to:

- the culture of the community;
- the culture of the school;
- the home life of the children.

It is important that we have a really good understanding of the community of which the school is a part. Children who experience contradictory cultures may find it very difficult to adapt to the changes they have to make from one to another. However, it is possible for the culture of the classroom to have an impact on the cultures outside it. From little acorns giant oak trees grow.

> **To sum up so far**
>
> ● What is the culture of your classroom like?
>
> ● Is it positive? Is it safe? Do children feel secure?
>
> ● Would the children give the same answers to these questions?

If the answer to these questions is yes then the rest of the ideas in this book are for you. First we will look at the steps involved in designing your own class activities before going on to look at some pre-existing structures that can be helpful.

A step-by-step guide to designing activities

We will look at five steps in the process of designing activities:

1　Pre-planning.

2　Audit of resources.

3　Mapping the learning experience.

4　Monitoring, assessment and evaluation

5　Designing the learning experience.

1 Pre-planning

Building in a sense of agency from the beginning is the first stage in the process, and needs to take place in plenty of time to allow the information to be gathered and the actual planning and design to be carried out. There are some questions to consider and three main things to do at the pre-planning stage.

Questions to ask yourself:

> ● Is it possible to offer the class a range of topics from which to choose or are we compelled to do a particular one? How interested in the topic are they? (It is likely that they will be more interested if they have had some involvement in choosing it.)
>
> ● What do they already know about the topic?
>
> ● Do they have any resources they could contribute?
>
> ● What would they like to learn more about?
>
> ● What do they want to get out of this learning experience? What aspects of their work might they like to concentrate on developing?

Things to do at the pre-planning stage:

- Involve the children in shaping the lesson, project or unit by negotiating the aims and content of learning with them.

- Take account of the knowledge and expertise that they already have. You can do this by gathering information from the children and their parents.

- Create a 'map' of what is known already and what is still to be learned.

2 Audit of resources

This is making sure that agency is possible. Building a sense of agency can falter if insufficient and inappropriate resources have been made available to the pupils. Often the variety of resources used by pupils is narrow. Teachers complain that the pupil 'simply downloaded it off the internet'. To help widen the range of resources consulted and utilised specific assessment criteria can be negotiated with the pupils. If greater credit is given to variety then pupils can be encouraged to look further afield for information.

Of course pupils themselves should be encouraged to identify, locate and access resources for themselves but it is especially important to see the pupils themselves as a resource. Many may already hold vast amounts of knowledge about a topic and this should be assessed and acknowledged as a resource in itself.

Questions to ask yourself:

- What can I make available from within the class or school?

- What have the pupils access to outwith school, e.g. at home? And do all pupils have equal access to this? If not how can it be shared?

- Can resources be made available from elsewhere, e.g. guest speakers from the local community?

- What sort of resources might be available to me?

- Is it possible to undertake visits?

Things to do when auditing resources:

- Involve the learners in gathering and providing resources where they can.

- Consider classroom, whole school, education authority and local community opportunities for challenge and sources of support.

- Create an inventory of all the possible resources that are at your disposal and the accessibility of these for all the children in the class. Some resources, for example, may only be accessible to some children with support.

- Identify any additional resources that require to be created, e.g. support sheets; activity sheets; reflection sheets etc., purchased, e.g. visual aids; games; books etc or organised, e.g. visits; guest speakers etc.

- Consider the role of professionals and other adults involved in the learning process, e.g. teaching assistants, parents etc.

3 Mapping the learning experience

This is the point where you take what is known and match it to what is required to be taught and what the pupils have identified that they would like to learn. From this teaching 'chunks' can be identified.

Questions to ask yourself:

- How long do we have and how long might this take? Are there compromises necessary?

- Do we have or can we at least identify where to get the resources that we need?

- Is there flexibility to allow pupils to plan their own learning pathways to some degree?

Things to do at the mapping stage:

- Use the map of what is known and what is to be learned to identify appropriate teaching chunks.

- Match the resources from the inventory to the teaching chunks on the map.

- Consider the teaching sequence or route. Is it possible for children to work through the activities in different orders? Are there times where the whole class or groups has/have to be together? Apply the possible sequences to the map to form a general plan.

- Create a timeline for the work to be completed. It is useful if all dates and times are a matter of negotiation (within the set framework) with extensions available.

4 Monitoring, assessment and evaluation

This is about building in opportunities for reflection. Assessment should always mirror the criteria negotiated with the learners at the pre-planning stage. It is often through ongoing, informal assessment that the most useful information can be gathered and indeed where the most powerful learning experiences can occur.

Questions to ask yourself:

- How will the children know if they have developed the aspects of their work that they identified in the pre-planning stage or not? Are the pupils clear about what the assessment criteria and format will be? What criteria would they use to judge their progress? What criteria would I use to judge progress? Is there agreement? How can they best record their progress and significant achievement?

- Where are the opportunities for me to observe, question and discuss with pupils their choice of tasks as well as their progress on the tasks and activities? This may involve planning for group discussions, reviewing pupils' notes and written work at set times, creating a timetable for pupils to make interim presentations of completed work to others in the class etc.

- How might I best offer feedback on their achievements: at what points (throughout, in the middle and/or at the end?), by what means (tests, observation, interview, oral questioning etc) and in what formats (verbal, written comment, grades and/or marks)?

- Are there to be opportunities for self and peer assessment? What weight should be given to these forms of assessment?

- How will the lesson, unit, project itself be evaluated?

Things to do in monitoring, assessment and evaluation:

- Involve the learners in agreeing the assessment criteria by which they and you will judge their progress.

- Build in opportunities for peer and self-assessment.

- Identify opportunities for you to assess and give feedback to pupils both individually and in groups.

5 Designing the learning experience

Building in opportunities for reflection and collaboration: now that all the preparation has been done we need to design the learning experience itself.

Questions to ask yourself:

- How and when might the children be involved in sharing the knowledge and understanding they already hold with others in the class? This might involve a child writing or recording information for others to read and comment on; presenting information to a group or the class; bringing in a resource for others to use or designing an activity for others to undertake.

- What is the best way of organising the pupils for this particular activity?

- Is there a range of ways in which pupils can access and offer knowledge and understanding – class lessons, group lessons, reading, writing, listening, watching, discussing, presentations?

- Where will the children get the time to prepare for their involvement?

- How might they best record their own aims and achievements for the learning experience?

- Can they be involved in peer assessment – where and how? Do they need support to do this?

Things to do at the design stage:

- Involve the learners in designing and delivering the lesson, project or unit by using the plan to identify individuals and groups to design, produce and share their knowledge of different sections with others.

- Agree learning targets, routes and assessment criteria with the learners. Negotiate with the children how, when and by what means learning will be assessed. Build in self and peer support and assessment systems.

- Identify where a choice of activities and content is possible and create a menu from which children can choose learning activities.

- Ensure that content, tasks and activities have an open-ended element so that achievement is not limited.

- Build in opportunities for individual, group and class work where possible. Consider which form of pupil organisation is best for particular activities, e.g. interest, ability, mixed ability, friendship, age and stage related, cross age and stage etc.

- Identify opportunities for links with learning taking place elsewhere.

- Consider how and what kinds of support can be provided to individuals through school staff, resources, peers and home.

Frameworks for improving the level of challenge and pupil interaction

The rest of this book offers some suggestions of how individual tasks might be designed in order to offer choice, agency, collaboration and reflection to all pupils. Chapter 3 looks at the sorts of questions that we can ask and encourage children to pose in order to raise the level of difficulty for those children who require more challenging activities. Chapter 4 looks at how providing menus of activities can mean that children have choice from a range of graded activities. Finally Chapter 5 offers a framework for a research project that incorporates both menus and higher order questioning as a way of providing opportunities for all children in the class to take part in the same project.

Points for reflection

- To what extent do you feel supported by a multi-layered system? How does this impact on what you are able to provide in the classroom?

- What is the culture of your classroom like? Are there aspects that need attention?

- To what extent do you go through all five steps when designing an activity? Do the activities you design provide opportunities for reflection, collaboration and agency?

Chapter 3

Asking Better Questions

In this chapter we will look at:

- What we know about questions.

- Seven different frameworks that can help us to ask the right sorts of questions.

What do we know about questions?

The best questions are ones which:

- stimulate children to want to answer them;

- do not require restricted, correct responses;

- encourage deep thinking and engagement with the problem.

It is all too easy, in the busy primary classroom, to find ourselves falling back on a narrow range of question types. In general we want to try to use the right kind of question at the right time. Whilst it is possible to categorise question types in a variety of different ways, I am going to stick to two broad categories: **closed** and **open**.

Closed questions tend to be good for checking and encouraging the recall of knowledge:

- finding out what facts are already known;

- finding out which facts have been remembered from teaching;

- directing children to specific information in a text;

- highlighting key points in a passage or presentation;

- helping children to make notes and summarise lessons;

- identifying gaps and difficulties in knowledge and understanding;

- leading into new learning.

Open questions are necessary if we want to help children think about ideas and topics by:

- stimulating ideas;

- focusing attention;

- stimulating curiosity and interest;

- stimulating discussion;

- eliciting views;

- identifying previous experiences and knowledge;

- recognising feelings;

- encouraging hard thinking;

- extending and deepening a topic.

One way to help us make sure that a range of questions are posed and that different questions are posed for different purposes is to use tried and tested frameworks to help us. Such frameworks can be useful for both teachers and pupils by helping to:

- reflect on topics that are being studied;

- examine the quality of questions that can be raised on a topic;

- offer a degree of choice in the questions that are to be tackled;

- create opportunities to work with more expert others in the close examination of a topic;

- create a range of questions on topics;

- offer specific types of questions for different purposes.

It is important that children understand the nature of questions and how different types of questions will require different types of answers. Encourage learners to ask more in-depth and probing questions by discussing what makes a good question. For example, each class can have a question post-box into which learners post questions as they occur to them. At the end of the day/week the post-box can be emptied and the questions can be analysed through posing questions about questions.

Questions about questions:

- Which questions are you most interested in hearing the answer to?

- Does it make you want to try to answer it yourself?

- Does it ask one thing or more than one thing?

- Is it long and complicated or short and simple?

- Is it asking something where the answer already exists?

- Does it have one answer or could there be lots of answers?

- Does it need a long or a short answer?

- Is the answer likely to be simple or difficult to find?

- Can one person answer it or will it need a group effort?

- What would be the best way to provide the answer or a response to the question (written, diagram, verbal, discussion, play etc)?

- Does it need a lot of work before an answer can be given? What kind of work is needed (research, thinking, talking etc)?

At the end of the analysis the children can identify which questions they think are the best and these can become the stimulus for further activities for individuals, groups or the whole class. We can also encourage children to become more independent by moving through stages of dependence[i].

Stages of dependence

- The pupils are directed to particular questions from the menu.

- The pupils choose from the menu.

- The pupils choose from the menu but also generate other examples of questions within the framework.

- The pupils use the framework to create their own menu of questions or indeed create their own framework.

Framework one: Benjamin Bloom's taxonomy[ii]

Bloom's taxonomy classifies thinking into a hierarchical order according to level of difficulty. Bloom suggested that the first three, knowledge, understanding and comprehension, constituted lower order skills and that more challenge was involved if learners were asked to engage with the last three: analysis, synthesis and evaluation.

The advantage that Bloom's taxonomy has over the other frameworks is that it offers a hierarchy of activities rather than a range of activities all at the same level.

Example: Jack and the beanstalk	
Knowledge	(remembering and retaining) What did Jack swap the cow for?
Comprehension	(interpreting and understanding) Why did Jack get into trouble from his mum for swapping the cow for the beans?
Application	(making use of) What would your mum say if you went for the shopping with £20 and came home with magic beans instead?
Analysis	(taking apart) List each of the characters in the story and what they do in the story
Synthesis	(putting together) If there had been a dragon living at the top of the beanstalk instead of a giant how might things have been different?
Evaluation	(judging and assessing) Was Jack a hero or a thief?

Thinking triangles

Using Bloom's taxonomy we can also create thinking triangles for each level in the taxonomy. A triangle can be at any of the six levels.

Thinking triangles can be useful frameworks to help pupils when they encounter new concepts, ideas or topics. Each triangle involves the same teacher input until the pupils are used to the approach.

Teacher input:

1   Explain the four aspects of the concept that have to be considered.

2   Use an easy word or concept to illustrate how it works.

3   Organise the pupils to work in pairs or small groups.

4   Provide a whole class opportunity for the pupils to bring all the triangles back to the larger group at the end.

5   Encourage the pupils to make up a triangle for someone else in their group to work on.

The example in Diagram 3.1 shows a **knowledge** triangle on volcanoes. As many triangles as necessary can be created at each level.

Diagram 3.1 **Example of a knowledge triangle**

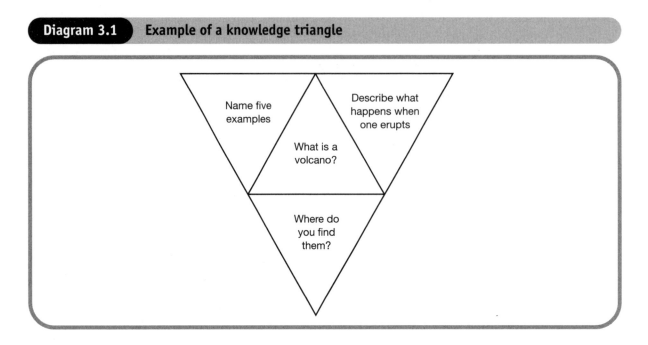

Triangles can also be created for any level of Bloom's taxonomy (see an example for the topic of volcanoes in Diagram 3.2). Once pupils have completed their answers they can bring them together to form a thinking hexagon. A completed hexagon provides the whole class with a useful summary of a topic.

● Framework two: Howard Gardner's multiple intelligences[iii]

Howard Gardner proposed a theory of **multiple intelligences** and views all abilities including those utilised in creative and aesthetic areas of the curriculum as fully cognitive:

no less cognitive than the skills of mathematicians and scientists.[iv]

It was his interest in recent developments and understandings of neuroscience that led Gardner into the study of neuropsychology. He studied with people who had brain damage through strokes and found that different human abilities are, in fact, different and distinct faculties of the brain. A person's strength in one area of performance does not predict any comparable strength in any other areas. He concluded that

the human mind is better thought of as a series of relatively separate faculties, with only loose and nonpredictable relations with one another, than as a single, all-purpose machine that performs steadily at a certain horsepower, independent of content and context.[v]

Diagram 3.2   **Example of a thinking hexagon**

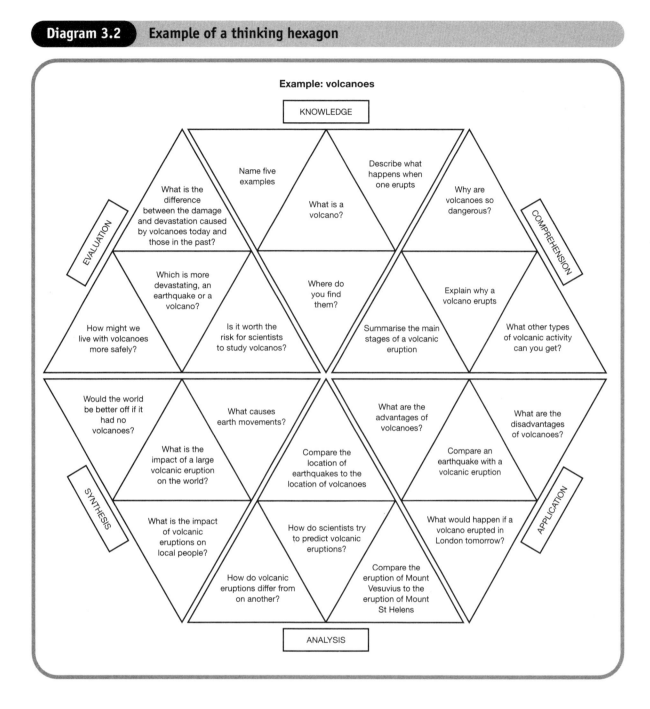

Example: volcanoes

KNOWLEDGE

EVALUATION

COMPREHENSION

SYNTHESIS

APPLICATION

ANALYSIS

- Name five examples
- Describe what happens when one erupts
- What is the difference between the damage and devastation caused by volcanoes today and those in the past?
- What is a volcano?
- Why are volcanoes so dangerous?
- Which is more devastating, an earthquake or a volcano?
- Where do you find them?
- Explain why a volcano erupts
- How might we live with volcanoes more safely?
- Is it worth the risk for scientists to study volcanos?
- Summarise the main stages of a volcanic eruption
- What other types of volcanic activity can you get?
- Would the world be better off if it had no volcanoes?
- What causes earth movements?
- What are the advantages of volcanoes?
- What are the disadvantages of volcanoes?
- What is the impact of a large volcanic eruption on the world?
- Compare the location of earthquakes to the location of volcanoes
- Compare an earthquake with a volcanic eruption
- What is the impact of volcanic eruptions on local people?
- How do scientists try to predict volcanic eruptions?
- What would happen if a volcano erupted in London tomorrow?
- How do volcanic eruptions differ from on another?
- Compare the eruption of Mount Vesuvius to the eruption of Mount St Helens

If, Gardner argues, all faculties are cognitive in origin then we should call them all the same thing, i.e. all abilities or all intelligences, but that there is no rationale which can justify separate terms for the different faculties of the brain. Gardner, very honestly, suggests that if he were to have called his book 'seven human gifts' it would have attracted little attention and voices concern at the power such labelling can have.

Gardner argues that intelligences are not things – that is, the word cannot be a noun – they are neural potentials which may or may not be activated depending upon the values and opportunities available to an individual within the culture in which he or she lives.

Rather than use the psychometric tradition to investigate the nature of intelligence Gardner laid out a set of eight separate criteria for intelligence to exist. If a candidate met the criteria reasonably well it was classified as an intelligence. These criteria came from different disciplinary roots. From the biological sciences: the potential of isolation by brain damage and an evolutionary history and evolutionary plausibility. From logical analysis: an identifiable core operation or set of operations and susceptibility to encoding in a symbol system. From developmental psychology: a distinct developmental history, along with a definable set of expert 'end state' performances and the existence of idiot savants, prodigies and other exceptional people. From traditional psychology: support from experimental psychological tasks and support from psychometric findings.

From this Gardner, originally, identified seven intelligences:

- verbal/linguistic;
- logical/mathematical;
- musical;
- bodily/kinaesthetic;
- visual/spatial;
- interpersonal;
- intrapersonal.

Gardner believes that each individual person's profile of intelligences will be different. He claims we all receive these intelligences as part of our birthright; no two people have exactly the same intelligences in the same combinations. After all,

> *intelligences arise from the combination of a person's genetic heritage and life conditions in a given culture and era.*[vi]

Gardner suggests well known people who demonstrate different intelligences to a high degree:

- Albert Einstein – logical mathematical;
- Sigmond Freud – intrapersonal;
- Mahatma Gandhi – interpersonal;
- Martha Graham – bodily kinaesthetic;
- Ludwig Van Beethoven – musical;
- Pablo Picasso – spatial;
- T S Eliot – linguistic.

If we all have a unique blend of intelligences then there is a challenge to education for the future – how do we take advantage of the uniqueness, which as a species we exhibit in having several intelligences?

Gardner makes a very important point: intelligences are neither good nor bad. No intelligence, in itself, is moral or immoral. They are, in fact, amoral and can, as such, be put to a constructive or a destructive use. In this respect we could acknowledge Hitler as being a genius in the area of interpersonal intelligence because of his abilities to manipulate and lead a nation.

Since his formulation of the original intelligences Gardner has more recently suggested that there may be more than seven. He has added a naturalist intelligence to the list but is still debating whether spiritual and/or existential should be included. At present he is

willing...to joke about 8½ intelligences.[vii]

Multiple intelligences can be used to ensure that a range of different activities are encouraged and that pupils have the opportunities to demonstrate and develop all their intelligences.

Example: looking at a story	
Verbal/linguistic	Choose a section from the story and prepare to read it aloud to the class. You may wish to include voices, sound effects, music etc.
	Rewrite the ending
	Rewrite the story as a horror story/fairy tale/thriller/romance...
	Compare this story to another that you have read which deals with the same topics/issues.
	Compare this story to another you have read by the same author.
	Choose a character from the story and write another story with the same character as the lead.
	Turn the story into a film script.
Mathematical/ logical	Create a board game based on the story. Make a flow diagram outlining the major steps of the plot.
Musical	Compose or find a theme tune/musical score for the story.
Bodily/kinaesthetic	Could this story be told through dance? What kind of dance would it be? See if you can create a dance that would tell part of the story.
Visual/spatial	Design a front cover for the story. Design a story board so that the story can be turned into a film.

▶

	Design a costume for one of the characters and say at which point in the story they would wear it. Explain why you designed the costume this way and be clear about the image you are trying to create.
Intrapersonal	How did this story affect you personally? Were there points when you felt sad, excited, angry etc? Why was this?
Interpersonal	If you were to prepare this story for stage or screen, how and at what points in the story would you create different moods for the audience?
Naturalistic	Organise and group the characters in a way that shows how they are related to one another and how they relate to one another in the story.

Framework three: Alex Osborn's SCAMPER checklist[viii]

SCAMPER is an acronym that stands for:

- Substitute

- Combine

- Adapt

- Modify

- Put to use

- Eliminate

- Reverse

Take, for example, playing a piece of music. The SCAMPER checklist would let children develop some ideas from the original piece.

Substitute	Choose (a) different instrument/s and play the piece of music again.
Combine	Put words to the music by choosing a poem to accompany it. Find someone to sing the new song.
Adapt	Play the piece in a different style e.g. pop, jazz, classical, blues, rock and roll etc.
Modify	Play the piece at a different tempo or with different emphasis.
Put to use	How could this piece of music be made use of in television or film?
Eliminate	Play only every second note. How does it sound?
Reverse	Play the music backwards. What difference does this make?

Teachers and pupils can also use this checklist to think about a story. This can be a really good exercise to help pupils let their imagination run riot.

Framework four: Joan Dalton's divergent questioning[ix]

This is a series of six open questions that encourage children to think about topics in a slightly different way. The questions are formulated around the following ideas:

- quantity;

- change;

- prediction;

- points of view;

- comparative association;

- and valuing.

Questions can be made up based on these ideas and then applied to almost any passage or topic. Take for example the following short passage about Scott of Antarctica.

Captain Robert Scott and his party of five left base camp in Antarctica in October 1911 with motor sledges, ponies and dogs in their bid to be the first at the South Pole. The motors soon broke down. The ponies, unable to cope with the extreme cold, were shot and the dogs sent back to base because Scott was unwilling to sacrifice them. The polar party, pulling sleds, arrived at the South Pole in January 1912 to find Amundson had already been there.

The weather on the return journey was exceptionally bad. Evans, the group doctor, died and Captain Oates sacrificed himself by walking out into a blizzard while his companions slept. The three survivors struggled on but were confined at their next camp for nine days by the blizzard and all perished. Their frozen bodies were found by search parties in November 1912.

Quantity	How many different ways can the South Pole be reached? Consider the possible sizes of groups which could take on this challenge. What is the optimum size and composition of such a group?
Change	Assume the doctor did not die first. Rewrite the story.
Prediction	If the blizzard had not kept them at camp for nine days on the way back how might things have been different?

►

Points of view	Write the story from the perspective of Captain Scott. Why might Captain Scott have been reluctant to sacrifice the dogs? Write the story from the point of view of one of the ponies.
Personal involvement	You were one of the party. Describe your journey and suggest things that you would have done differently.
Comparative association	Compare an expedition in Antarctica with one in a tropical rainforest. Compare an expedition today with the one in 1912.
Valuing	Was Captain Oates right to take his own life?

⬤ Framework five: Reciprocal teaching[x]

The original work by Palinscar and Brown (1984) suggests a four-stage strategy to aid text comprehension and metacognition:

- clarify;

- question;

- summarise;

- predict.

Work carried out in Glasgow by support for learning teachers would suggest that a further two stages can be added to great effect. The key to reciprocal teaching is that at every step in the process children are encouraged to make explicit their strategies for understanding the text, problem, or topic.

The six steps involved are:

1   Clarify.

2   Question.

3   Summarise.

4   Predict.

5   Visualise – what do you 'see' when you read this text? Could it be presented differently, as a poster, film, graph etc?

6   Link – how does this link to what you know from other studies, readings etc?

Children should form study groups. Your own knowledge of the class will tell you what kinds of groups these should be. The format works equally well with mixed attainment groups as it does with similar attainment groups.

The children have to learn the process first and so have to be taught the steps to go through and what each means. Classroom assistants can be a great help when supporting a group to learn this strategy. In steps one and three where individual children take the lead it should be ensured that this role is not always undertaken by the same child. Let us look at the different steps and use studying a passage from a book as an example of what the group has been asked to do.

Step one: Clarify

This is the stage where we make sure that everyone in the group knows what it is that is to be studied. Some time is given for everyone to read over the passage to themselves. Someone in the group reads the passage aloud to the group. This can be particularly helpful for less secure readers who have sophisticated abilities in higher order skills. During this time the children may be:

- underlining or highlighting certain words that they do not know how to pronounce, that they do not understand and that are new to them;

- highlighting phrases that they particularly like or that they think are difficult to follow.

Step two: Question

This is the stage where the children are encouraged to ask questions or make statements about the text.

- Are there words that they have not come across before?

- Are there words they do not understand?

- Are there bits of the information that they do not understand?

- Is there any information that would have been helpful that is not provided in the passage?

- Do they like the way some phrases or sentences have been written? Why?

- Do they find the way some sentences have been written unhelpful? Why?

Each child should be encouraged to ask a question and the answers are discussed as a group. During this time the children are encouraged to be explicit about the strategies they use to help understand what it is they are reading. When I meet a word I do not understand, for example, I:

- read on and hope that it will come clear;

- may go back and read the bit before and after the word to see if I can begin to get a sense of what it means;

- may ask others what they think it means; I may also go to a dictionary;

- may use a thesaurus to give me other words (that I may be more familiar with) that have similar meaning;

This way I can build up a good sense of what the word means. I then try to check my full understanding by trying to use the word where possible in my own writing.

Step three: Summarise

Ask one of the group to say what they think the key points of the passage are.

- What are the facts being provided?

- What are the key events?

- Who are the key characters etc?

The group can then discuss whether or not this is too much information or too little. At the end of the discussion the group should have agreed what is a good summary of the key information in the passage.

Step four: Predict

The group should generate ideas and have a range of possible scenarios of what might happen next in the story. This way we can encourage pupils to see that the author had a choice about how the story would develop.

Step five: Visualise

This step can be particularly useful as a check to see if the children have understood the passage. It also encourages them to see how different people interpret the same story. The pupils should be asked to describe what they are visualising as they read the story:

- what the characters look like;

- what they are wearing;

- what the setting is like.

This aspect of the reciprocal reading process can lead into very useful discussions about the place of film in literature and how it can be both helpful and a hindrance to the interpretation of a story. There is great fun to be had trying to cast the story as a film using famous film stars or even the children in the class.

Step six: Link

Here the pupils get a chance to say how the story might link to

- their own personal experiences;

- other stories they have read;

● other stories by the same author;

● other information they might have about the theme or topic of the story.

Framework six: Critical thinking

This might be a useful framework for pupils to use when encountering new concepts. The model operates on the premise that learners develop understanding of new concepts by studying them in relation to other, more familiar, concepts. Pupils analyse four aspects of a concept or word doing four things.

1 What are the facts/is the evidence?
   a. What are the sources?
      i   Are they reliable?
      ii Are they relevant?
   b. Are they accurate and precise?
   c. Are they well defined?

2 Are they presented impartially?
   a. Is emotive language used?
   b. Does it appeal to emotions rather than reason?

3 Are the facts consistent with
   a. Other facts presented in the text?
   b. What you already know?
   c. Other points of view?
   d. Other sources?

4 Are there any inaccuracies or inconsistencies?

The following example is a newspaper article that appeared in a national paper entitled *Power Surge*.

Scottish Gas are the most expensive gas suppliers in the country – and they just got even dearer. The energy company – who make £1.5 million profit every day – have just decided to hike gas prices by more than 12 per cent, while putting up electricity charges by nearly 10 per cent. The news is a disaster for thousands of vulnerable customers who struggle to heat and light their homes. The company have blamed the rises on the high price of gas they pay. But come off it. When the price comes down again – as it surely will – will they cut charges to consumers? Don't hold your breath. Once again, these rises show the contempt energy companies have for their loyal customers. Energywatch Scotland are right to call for an investigation into how they operate. They are making a killing – at our expense.

1 What are the facts?

Scottish Gas are raising gas prices by 12% and electricity prices by nearly 10%.

2 Are they impartial?

No. It is clear from the articles that the writer disagrees strongly with the decision to raise prices. The language used in places is quite emotional, e.g. 'come off it' and 'don't hold your breath'. The author also offers an opinion, i.e. 'They are making a killing – at our expense.'

3 Are they consistent?

The article is consistently critical of the Scottish Gas position.

4 Are there inaccuracies?

Electricity prices are said to rise by 'nearly 8%' but the actual figure is not stated. Does this mean 8% or 9%? It is not clear.

Framework seven: Self-reflection

In Chapter 2 we looked at the need for reflection in the learning process to encourage what Jerome Bruner describes as 'going meta' (it is more properly known as metacognition). Choosing from and adding to the following list of questions might help pupils do exactly this. In Chapter 5 we use some of these questions to form a self-assessment sheet related to project work.

Self-reflection questions

What did I learn about:

- The topic?
- My feelings?
- Other people in the group?

How did I find the work?

- What were the easiest bits?
- What were the hardest bits?
- What were the most enjoyable bits?
- What were the least enjoyable bits?

How do I feel about the work?

- What do I feel confident about?
- What do I know and understand?
- What am I not so confident about?
- What would I like to learn more about?

How did I manage to:

- Work through hard bits?
- Maintain interest when things were easy?
- Keep going when things were not enjoyable or hard?

What did I think of:

- The topic?
- My own work?
- The work of others in the group?

How did I behave?

- Was I helpful to others?
- Was I patient with others?
- Was I polite and courteous to others?
- Did I concentrate well?
- Did I cover a lot of work?

How do I like to learn?

- I like to read about things.
- I like to listen.
- I like to watch.
- I like doing things.
- Something else?

How do I *not* like to learn?

- I don't like reading.
- I don't like listening.
- I don't like watching.

- I don't like taking part in things.
- Something else?

Points for relection

- Asking more open and stimulating questions allows pupils to more freely demonstrate and develop their abilities.
- Frameworks can help us as teachers to extend the range of questions that we regularly use in class.
- All the frameworks encourage active engagement with a topic by promoting creative and critical thinking that all pupils can engage with.
- Pupils themselves should be encouraged to use, develop and create frameworks which can help them to investigate topics.

Chapter 4

The Menu Approach

In this chapter we will:

- Think about the issue of choice as a way of motivating pupils and promoting independent learning.

- Consider the use of menus in a range of subject areas based on a framework of three levels of challenge.

It is suggested that a menu of activities can be created that allows learners to develop their understanding of a topic based on the multiple intelligences theory. Once again this approach offers opportunities to:

1   Reflect on topics that are being studied.

2   Offer opportunities for self-direction in the activities that are to be tackled.

3   Work with more expert others in the close examination of a topic.

The menu approach is a very simple idea based on providing a list of activities of various different kinds and/or of varying forms of participation. Three forms of participation are suggested here:

- involvement

- development

- creation.

It may be that individually learners can only choose from the involvement list, but working with others they can take part in activities from the development list. Equally some children may be able to work individually from the development list but with the support of others also work with the creation list. Finally, there will be children who can work at all three levels independently but can be encouraged to push the boundaries of their abilities by working within a group.

Examples are provided for English language (stories and poems); science; geography; and maths.

Involvement

- **Summarising:** what are the key points? What are the most important messages/themes?

- **Identifying:** make a list of features/characters.

- **Explaining:** how does this work? Why does this happen?

- **Setting:** what is the background to this? Make up questions about this topic.

- **Visualising:** how do you imagine this? What might this look like? Can this be shown as a picture or diagram?

- **Demonstrating:** show others how you do this. Demonstrate how this might happen.

- **Presenting:** explain your views/work/findings to others.

- **Defining:** what is meant by this word or term? Find out more about…

- **Rethinking or reinterpreting:** are there other ways of looking at this? Are there other ways of showing this? Are there other ways of presenting this?

- **Interpreting:** what do you think this means? What is the importance of…?

Development

- **Alternatives:** are there other ways of getting the same answer? Are there other answers one could get? How else might this be achieved? Are there different approaches that might work?

- **Futures:** what was this the start or beginning of? What did this lead to?

- **Prequels:** what happened before? What led to this?

- **Sequels:** what happened after? What were the consequences? What might happen next?

- **Introduce:** if you add novelty/something new what difference would it make?

- **Remove:** if you take away a key character/aspect/component what difference would it make?

- **Research:** find out some new information.

- **Reflect:** how does this make you feel? What have you learned from this? Does this link with anything else you already know? How did you do this? If you were to do this again would you do anything different?

- **Compare:** how does this compare to other things we know about? What are the similarities/differences between this and...

- **Develop:** write/rewrite your own version. How does this affect...? What is the longest/shortest/biggest/smallest...?

Creation

- **Design:** a (game/toy/appliance/tool/front cover...) to help take forward a particular project or problem.

- **Devise:** create special effects/a storyboard/ an experiment/a guide... to help clarify or illustrate a particular idea or issue.

- **Construct:** make a game/toy/appliance/tool/video... on a particular topic. Put together an argument for or against...

- **Invent:** another planet/a new animal/a machine/a symbol...

- **Compose:** write/select/choreograph/compose... a text/graph/diagram/piece of music/dance/poem/song ... to illustrate/enhance a project or idea.

- **Establish:** set up a group to look at/take action on a particular issue. Agree ground rules for an initiative.

- **Initiate:** organise a debate. Start a discussion forum. Agree and put in place changes to existing structures/arrangements. Try something new.

- **Produce:** a report or policy on an issue or topic of interest.

- **Generate:** suggestions/a list of examples. Write or direct your own version of the story/film/play/idea...

- **Formulate:** ideas to evaluate/assess how well a project/change/initiative has gone.

Example one: stories – *The Three Little Pigs*

Involvement

- Summarise the story in as few words as possible.

- Make a list of all the characters in the story and write a little bit about what you think of each of them. Who would you most like to be and why?

- Explain why a house made of bricks would be stronger than houses made of straw or sticks.

- Make up five questions on the story for others to answer.

- Visualise the point in the story where the wolf blows down the house made of straw. Make a drawing to show your idea of what this would look like to the class.

- Demonstrate how a house made of straw could be made stronger.

- Present your views of the story to the class.

- Find out what you can about wolves. How like a real wolf is the one in the story?

- Present the story as a cartoon strip.

- What message might the story hold for the reader?

Development

- The story was called *The Three Little Pigs*. What would you have called it?

- What do you think happens to the three little pigs after the story ends?

- What brought the wolf to the three little pigs' houses?

- How might other wolves be affected by what the pigs did?

- What would have happened if there had been a farmer in the story?

- If there had only been two little pigs how might the story have been different?

- Ask the other children in your class which character they liked best in the story and why.

- If you had been the wolf what would you have done?

- Compare this story to the story of Little Red Riding Hood.

- Rewrite the story as a horror story.

Creation

- Design a front cover for the storybook of *The Three Little Pigs*.

- Devise special effects to create different moods while the story is being read aloud.

- Make a board game or video based on the story.

- Invent a machine that would blow down a house made of bricks.

- Compose a report; piece of music; poem; or song about the story.

- Set up a story club in the class or in the school to discuss stories like this one.

- Identify any messages the story might have for readers and hold a class debate on the issues.

- Produce a news report for radio about what happened to the little pigs and to the wolf.

- Write your own story about building a house.

- Create five criteria which you would use to judge the quality of a fable or fairy story.

Example two: poetry – 'The Tyger' by William Blake

Involvement

- Summarise what the poem is about in as few words as possible.

- List all the words that the poet uses to describe the tiger.

- Explain why you think that William Blake uses a blacksmith's workshop and tools to help describe the tiger.

- Make up five questions for others to answer about the poem.

- Imagine a tiger being created in a blacksmith's workshop. Draw a picture to show your thoughts.

- Demonstrate to others in the class how a tiger moves.

- Prepare a poster to present information on tigers to others in the class.

- Rewrite the poem as a newspaper article.

- What do you think William Blake thought of tigers?

Development

- Think of as many other titles for this poem as you can.

- Tigers are an endangered species. Find out why and whether extinction is inevitable or not.

- Why do you think tigers exist? What is their purpose? Are they useful creatures or not?

- What do you think happened to this tiger after William Blake wrote his poem?

- Think of a tiger cub. How might it be described? Would you describe it in the same way as William Blake described its parent? If not why not and how would you describe it?

- William Blake gives us a picture of a tiger being made in a blacksmith's workshop. How else could a tiger be made in order to give the reader an impression of strength and power?

- Research and compile a list of other poems about cats.

- How did the poem make you feel about tigers? Why do you think it had that effect?

- Compare a tiger with a pet cat.

- Write your own poem about a tiger.

Creation

- Design a poster to advertise the poem.

- Devise a storyboard for a piece of film that could accompany the reading of the poem.

- Put together a book of poems about cats for a younger class. Include original poems by yourself and/or others in your class as well as published poems.

- Invent a new animal even more powerful than a tiger.

- Compose background music that could be played while the poem is read aloud.

- Establish a poetry group in your class/school and use 'The Tyger' as your first poem for discussion.

- Initiate a debate in the school on endangered species.

- Produce a presentation for the class on tigers.

- Choreograph a dance to accompany the reading of the poem.

- What makes a good poem? Make a list of things to look for.

Example three: science – space

Involvement

- Summarise the main points you have learned about space.

- Identify the nine planets in our solar system in order of distance from the sun.

- Explain to the class what effect our moon has on the Earth.

- How do stars, galaxies and constellations get their names?

- Visualise what the surface of Neptune might look like and draw a picture to show the rest of the class what you think.

- Demonstrate to the class, using a globe and a torch, why we experience different seasons in the United Kingdom.

- Present a lesson to the class on what Albert Einstein said about the speed of light.

- Define the following five key terms: solar; moon; planet; black hole; galaxy.

- What would happen if we found another planet that had gravity and a breathable atmosphere?

- What does the fact that life may exist on another planet mean for us on Earth?

Development

- What are the alternatives to using fossil fuels as an energy source for space rockets?

- What will space rockets look like in the future?

- How did life on Earth begin?

- How do you think life on Earth will evolve?

- What would happen to the planets in our solar system if we had two suns instead of one?

- What would happen to the planets in our solar system if the sun suddenly disappeared?

- Who do people in your class/school think is the most important scientist ever to have lived?

- Is space travel worth all the money and attention? Do you think that there is life on other planets? Why?/why not? If there is life on other planets would it be good to get in touch?

- Compare space travel with deep ocean exploration – which is most useful to mankind?

- Develop a calendar for a planet that takes 500 days to circle its sun.

Creation

- Design a space suit for astronauts travelling to Mars.

- Devise an experiment for the next Mars explorer to carry out.

- Put together an argument in defence of spending several billion pounds to develop space travel to Mars.

- You have been asked to invent a machine that can gather rock samples in zero gravity. Sketch out and annotate a design that might work.

- Compose or select music that should be played to any new life forms we meet in our travels in space.

- Set up a group from within the class to draw up guidelines for first contact with extra terrestrials.

- Start a discussion forum in the class/school to consider the moral implications of current scientific developments.

- Produce a report informing others in the class of the benefits we have all had from the space programme, e.g. non-stick pots and pans.

- Suggest as many other astrological symbols as you can by joining the stars in different ways.

- Create five criteria on which you would judge new discoveries and inventions related to space travel.

Example four: geography – tropical rainforests

Involvement

- Summarise and prioritise the safety considerations for anyone planning a trip to the rainforest.

- Identify the things that would be dangerous for people in a trip to the rainforest.

- Choose three plants or animals and explain how they have adapted to living in the rainforest.

- Set five question for others to answer about deforestation.

- What would the ideal clothing be for a trip into the rainforest? Draw a picture with notes to explain the features of each item. If you were to travel to the rainforest tomorrow what clothes (without buying new ones) do you have in your wardrobe that would be suitable? Bring them to school and explain why you think they are suitable.

- Demonstrate to the class how baskets are made by local people.

- Present a lecture/lesson/poster/play on the explorer David Livingstone.

- Define what these words mean: ecosystem; deforestation; parasite; tropical; extinction.

- The rainforests have been compared to a giant set of lungs. What do you think this means?

- Why do you think that the governments of places like Brazil have such a hard job trying to protect the rainforests?

Development

- If cars, boats and planes ran on sugar rather than oil what difference would it make to countries like Brazil? To help you, you may like to consider what life is like for oil rich countries today, e.g. Bahrain and Saudi Arabia. Would using sugar to fuel cars, trains and planes help save or help destroy the tropical rainforests?

- How might the climate of Britain be affected in the future by the destruction of the tropical rainforests?

- Oil is found in the tropical rainforests. How is oil formed?

- How are the lives of people living in the tropical rainforest going to change over the next 20 years?

- An animal that eats bromeliads (plants that provide a home to small amphibians, e.g. frogs and insects) is let lose in the rainforests. What difference will it make?

- If tigers became extinct in India what difference would it make?

- Find out the school's recycling policy. What does it do with paper, plastic and glass waste?

- If you could introduce one law to help save the rainforests, which all countries had to obey, what would it be? What would this law mean for the people who lived in the different countries most affected?

- Compare the tropical rainforests with the temperate rainforests.

- How are the industrial developments in the tropical rainforests helping the people who live there?

Creation

- Design your own eco-friendly hotel for tourists to visit the tropical rainforest. The hotel would have to blend in with its surroundings in the tropical rainforests and would have to cause as little disruption and damage to the plants and wildlife as possible. Think about the numbers of people that you would be able to cater for, what they would eat, how you would get supplies into the hotel and what would happen to any rubbish that is produced.

- Devise safety guides for people wishing to visit the tropical rainforests.

- Put together an argument in defence of spending several billion pounds to develop alternative energy sources.

- Invent a machine that can harvest coconuts safely.

- Write a letter to local companies asking them about their recycling policies.

- Set up an action group on tropical rainforests. How might such an action group make their opinions known and understood?

- Start a discussion forum in the class/school to consider the implications of current industrial development in the rainforests.

- Produce a policy for your school on recycling.

- Generate suggestions for how to improve recycling and conservation in the local area.

- Create five criteria on which you would judge new developments proposed for the rainforest areas.

Example five: maths – numbers

Involvement

- Summarise the main points of (Albert Einstein/Lord Kelvin/Sir Issac Newton's...) work.

- List as many scores as possible that you could get with three darts using a normal dartboard.

- What is a fraction?

- Set five questions for others in your class to answer about percentages.

- Julie wants to plant a tree exactly in the middle of her garden. How can she do this without measurement?

- Demonstrate how to work out whether a number is prime or not.

- Pick out the most interesting thing you know about numbers and tell the rest of the class.

- What is the binary system?

- Show as many two digit numbers as you can that have both vertical and horizontal symmetry.

- What are the five most important formulae ever developed? Why are these your top five?

Development

- You can get the answer 42 by multiplying 6×7 but there are lots of other ways of getting the answer 42 – think of as many ways as you can.

- Do prime numbers ever stop? What is the largest prime number you can find?

- Where do the words calculus, fraction and percentage come from?

- What is the newest development in mathematics?

- Introduce mathematical symbols to the following three numbers (5, 6, 7) to create the largest or smallest number you can.

- If you remove the brackets from an equation what difference does it make?

- Make up a questionnaire to find out what members of class think about numbers. Do they like them? Do they enjoy working out answers?

- What difference would it make to the world if we did not have numbers?

- You have a choice to be paid £200 a week or £5 an hour. What will influence your decision?

- What is the largest number you can write with four digits (hint: it is not 9999).

Creation

- Design a game to help younger children learn their tables.

- Devise a code using numbers so that you can send secret messages to your friends.

- Draw a graph to show the results of the research into class opinions of numbers.

- Invent a new mathematical symbol and try it out in a few calculations.

- Write a story about the number 0 (zero).

- Set up a 'we love numbers' group in your school to find out about fascinating facts about numbers.

- Organise a debate to decide the question: who was the greatest mathematician of all time?

- Make a book or web page of fascinating facts about numbers from the work of the 'we love numbers' group for others to access.

- Generate a list of examples from real life where the numbers have been important. Examples might be:
  - the use of the number seven in films (*The Magnificent Seven; The Seven Samurai*);
  - the number 13 is said to be unlucky – why is that?

- What makes a good number problem? Make a list of the types of problems that you enjoy trying to solve. Do they have some things in common?

Points for reflection

- Offering choice to pupils can be a way of providing a more motivating classroom environment and promoting independence in learning.

- Choice increases agency. In Chapter 2 we considered the importance of agency in creating a challenging classroom environment.

- Three levels of challenge – involvement, development and creation – can offer a range of pupils opportunities for interaction with similar subject matter.

Chapter 5

Managing Whole Class Research Projects

In this chapter we will:

- Think about the purpose of project work.

- Provide a five-step approach to project work.

- Think about ways of ensuring that all five steps are undertaken.

- Suggest ways of grouping pupils for project work.

- Consider tropical rainforests (TRF) as an example throughout this chapter.

- Suggest that class projects might have two parts to them, each of which concentrate on different steps within the five-step approach.

What is the purpose of project work?

Project work is an opportunity for children to investigate topics that are of genuine interest to them and which impact on their lives. The strength of project work is the fact that it is situated in real life. Whether it is an historical project (the Scottish Wars of Independence) or a contemporary topic (the disappearing tropical rainforests), they are researching about real people and real situations.

Project work is also an ideal way to support children as they move away from being information consumers, which requires little thought, imagination or skill, to being information producers[i]. Being an information producer requires children to learn to:

- take greater responsibility for their own learning;

- work with others as well as on their own;

- gather information and organise it for analysis;

- synthesise and draw conclusions based on evidence gathered;

- make moral and value judgements about key issues.

The various curriculum guidelines in the UK all suggest similar steps in project work. These steps relate to planning, collecting and recording evidence, interpreting and evaluating and presenting data. I have added one more step to the beginning of the process to take account, explicitly, of the knowledge that pupils already bring to the learning experience. In this way we have a five-step approach to project work.

- Step one: existing expertise.

- Step two: planning.

- Step three: collecting and recording evidence.

- Step four: interpreting and evaluating.

- Step five: presenting data.

Using these five steps effectively for whole class project work depends on:

1 How we value and encourage diversity.

2 How we group the pupils in the class.

3 Covering all five steps.

The tropical rainforests will be used throughout this chapter as an example.

1. How we value and encourage diversity

We tend to rely heavily in schools on reading for information and on prose for recording and presentation. Limiting the possibilities for access to information and limiting the possibilities for pupils to demonstrate what they know and can do excludes them from many activities and opportunities. Some gifted and talented pupils can have their abilities supressed by such limitations. Yet there are many ways in which pupils can, and should, be encouraged to engage with information and data.

Diversity of information gathering and recording techniques

- Information can be gleaned from the internet, DVDs, CD ROMs, maps, photographs, paintings, television, radio, video, video conferencing and talking books.

- Information can be recorded via CD, DVD, video or audiotape, diagrams, mindmaps, photographs, drawings and web pages.

Diversity of presenting techniques

The presentation of information to others often benefits from formats other than the written word. A recent candidate in the Masters programme at the university I work in presented an artefact[ii] as her final dissertation and gained a top award. Almost anything is possible. Final presentations of group work to the class can, therefore, benefit from variety:

- poems can be written;

- short plays can be performed;

- posters can be made;

- video doumentaries can be constructed;

- photograph collages made;

- images drawn, painted or moulded;

- a piece of work can be represented in an object which is made or assembled which represents the issues or points to be made. As it is said a picture, or in this case an object, paints a thousand words.

Opportunities in and from the wider community

- School trips can be a bonus to any project. Many botanic gardens, for example, do brilliant tours on all sorts of topics related to the rainforests.

- Outside speakers may be prepared to come into the school to add another viewpoint to issues being investigated.

- Pupils themselves will have ideas on who might speak and/or what visits might be undertaken. One of the pupils I worked with had a house full of tropical plants because his dad was a keen botanist. They only lived round the corner and so a short trip to his house for the group doing flora and fauna was quickly arranged. His dad very kindly took a day off work and talked to the group at length about the different plants he was gowing. He even lent some of his prize specimens to the group so that they could show the rest of the class.

2. How we group pupils in the class

Generally research projects involve children working individually, in pairs or in small groups and these are great ways of working. However, the most common approach is for everyone to investigate the same thing, for example, everyone in the class investigates tropical rainforests.

Having everyone in the class investigate the same thing restricts the class to a limited amount of information. When the children are asked to share what they have found they quickly become bored because they are sharing the same information: they have all become experts in the same general area. This is unlikely to happen in real life where experts in different fields come together in order to solve problems and identify ways forward.

Everyone in the class can be more profitably involved though the grouping and regrouping of pupils to build individual, paired, group and, finally, class expertise. When grouping children for project work prior expertise and skills should be taken into account as well as their specific interests. In this way, rather than everyone in the class investigating tropical rainforests, each group investigates a different aspect of tropical rainforests such as:

- location and climate;

- resources and industry;

- flora and fauna;

- people and ways of life.

A possible grouping arrangement for a class of 24 pupils might be four groups of six (see Diagram 5.1).

Diagram 5.1 **Pupil grouping for project work**

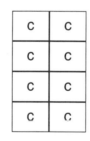
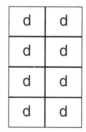

a	a	b	b	c	c	d	d
a	a	b	b	c	c	d	d
a	a	b	b	c	c	d	d
a	a	b	b	c	c	d	d

- group A may be investigating location and climate;
- group B may be investigating resources and industry;
- group C may be investigating flora and fauna;
- group D may be investigating people and ways of life.

3. Covering all five steps

Traditionally, class and individual research projects in schools have emphasised the collection and presentation of data. These aspects of project work are generally very well done. The aspects least well done, and yet, ironically, which lend themselves best to providing challenge for gifted pupils, are establishing existing expertise, planning and the interpretation and evaluation of data.

The stepped approach advocated by the curriculum outlines in the UK is a good one for making sure that every step is given due attention. In this approach children actively revise and rethink their research questions and plan as they work through the project. The more skilled the children become at research the less linear and more circular the process becomes. This has been summarised in Diagram 5.2.

Diagram 5.2 **The circular planning model**

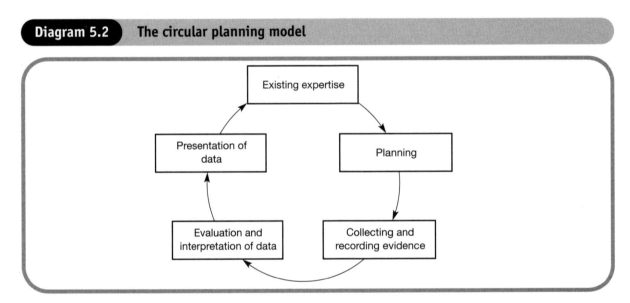

Giving pupils an overview of the project can be very helpful in providing the 'big picture' in what they are doing. Giving pupils the big picture helps them to:

- see what is being asked of them;
- see how this fits into the larger work of the class;
- gain an overview of the project.

An example of the big picture for our project on tropical rainforests (TRF) is provided on the next page. We will then go through each of the five steps in the project process in turn.

Topic: tropical rainforests
The Big Picture: Part one

This is a whole class research project about the tropical rainforests.

What you will be asked to do

- You will be asked to work as part of a group on one particular topic.
- You will decide with your teacher who will be in your group and which topic you should investigate
- You will be asked to go through five steps as part of your research.
- Once you have gathered all the information you can about your topic your group will be asked to organise this information and then present it to the rest of the class.

Topics for study

- Location and climate.
- Resources and industry.
- Flora and fauna.
- People and ways of life.

If you would like to add a topic to this list you should talk this over with your group and the teacher.

Steps of the project

Step one: What do we already know?

Step two: What do we need to think about and plan?

Step three: How will we collect and record information?

Step four: What does all this tell us?

Step five: How will we decide what to tell others and how will we do this?

The topic our group is going to study is _____

The members of our group are _____

_____

_____

Step one: existing expertise

It is important that pupils get a chance to share what they already know with their group. There is little point in them finding out the same information again. There may be information that they have that they:

- Know a lot about and with a good deal of certainty. This information should be noted for later use.

- Know a bit about but are unsure of the accuracy of the information. This should form the basis of questions that they would wish to investigate.

- Know nothing about. The teacher may have to support and direct the pupils to these areas.

Question for the pupils to consider:

- What do you already know about the topic that is useful?

Step two: planning

What does planning involve for the pupils?

- Negotiating which aspect of the project to investigate.

- Raising questions related to the topic.

- Deciding on strategies, procedures, sources and resources:
    - What kind of information do I need to collect?
    - Where can I get the information I need?
    - How do I collect people's views?
    - How do I gather factual data?
    - What materials and/or equipment do I need?

- Justifying choices:
    - How will this information answer my question/s?
    - Why are these the best ways of collecting the information I need?
    - What is wrong with the other ways of collecting information?
    - Why is this the best information and why am I not using other information?

- Monitoring for possible bias:
    - Does the information I have collected represent particular views or attitudes?
    - Are there alternative/opposing viewpoints that I need to take into account?

- Deciding on a sequence of tasks:
  - What should I do first and why?

- Presenting group plans to the whole class (e.g. each group in turn presents their plan to the whole class).

A photocopiable planning sheet has been provided (page 70) for use by pupils, as have some completed thinking hexagons (Diagrams 5.3 to 5.6) on four sub-topics of tropical rainforests which may assist some pupils who have difficulty in generating their own questions. The four sub-topics provided are:

- location and climate;

- resources and industry;

- flora and fauna;

- people and ways of life.

You may wish to give particularly gifted pupils the opportunity to make up their own thinking hexagons.

Questions for the pupils to consider:

- Do you need to find out any more about the topic?

- How will you find this out?

Step three: collecting and recording evidence

What does collecting evidence involve for the pupils?

Methods of collecting the information

1 Interview a set number of people face to face.

2 Phone key people.

3 Post out or deliver a questionnaire or letters.

4 Search the internet, use DVDs or CD ROMs.

5 Read books, articles or newspapers.

6 Watch TV or video programmes.

7 Listen to radio programmes.

Planning Sheet

Name of the group _____

1   Which area of interest have you agreed to investigate?

2   What do you already know that is useful? You may wish to attach a record of what you already know to this planning sheet

3   What sorts of things do you want to find out? What questions do you want to answer? (Use, adapt or create a thinking hexagon to help you.)

4   Where and how will you find this information?

5   How will you record the information?

6   What equipment or materials might you need?

7   Who will do what?

Once you have collected and recorded all your information use this next section to help you plan further.

1   What can you say about the topic or issue now? This information will be recorded elsewhere but you may wish to attach a summary of the main points you want to tell others about.

2   How will you present your ideas to other people?

3   Who will do what?

Diagram 5.3 Thinking hexagon for studying the location and climate of the tropical rainforests

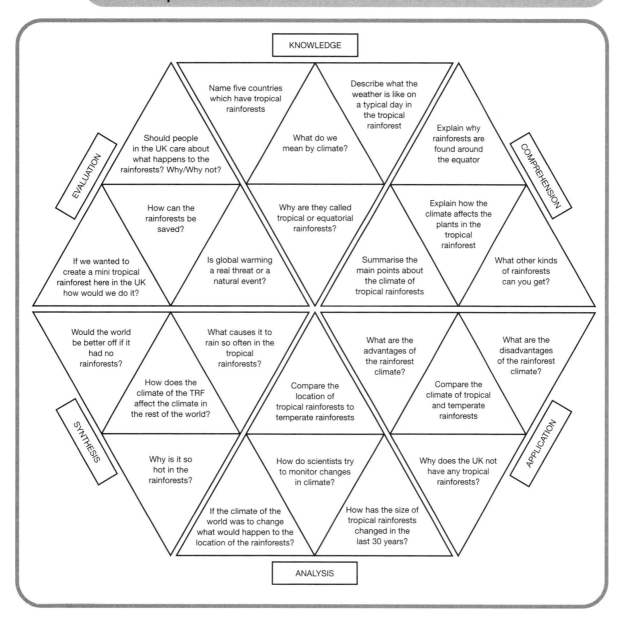

Choosing, adapting or designing the collection instrument that will be used:

1 A letter.

2 A questionnaire.

3 An interview schedule.

4 An observation schedule.

5 An outline for recording notes.

What does recording evidence involve for the pupils?

Diagram 5.4 **Thinking hexagon for studying the resources and industry of the tropical rainforests**

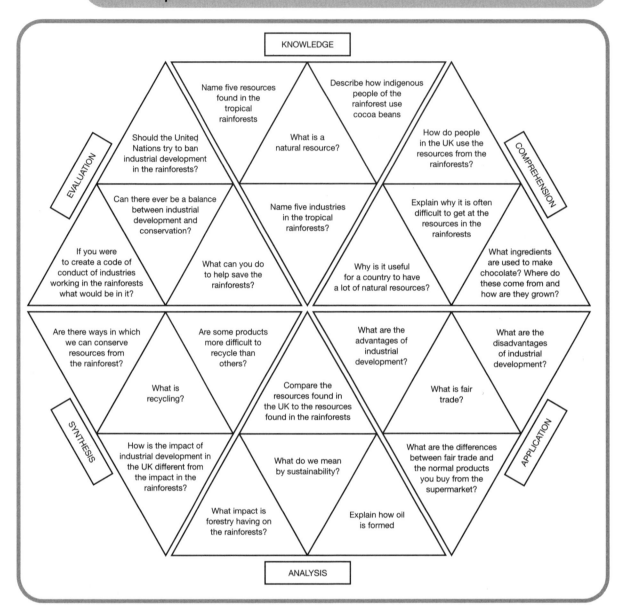

Methods of recording the information collected:

1 Summarise key information that has been read or heard.

2 Take notes from books or interviews.

3 Use ICT, e.g. databases.

4 Use notation diagrams, graphs and symbols.

5 Design and use data collection sheets, e.g. observation, controlled experiments, data logging, questionnaires and surveys.

6 Video, tape, DVD or CD recording.

7 Photographs.

8 Drawings and/or sketches.

9 Plans or maps.

10 Mind maps.

Once the information is collected it is a good idea to present it to the group.

Clearly some of the ways of collecting and recording information will be dictated by the resources that the teacher and the pupils have available to them.

| Diagram 5.5 | **Thinking hexagon for studying the flora and fauna of the tropical rainforests** |

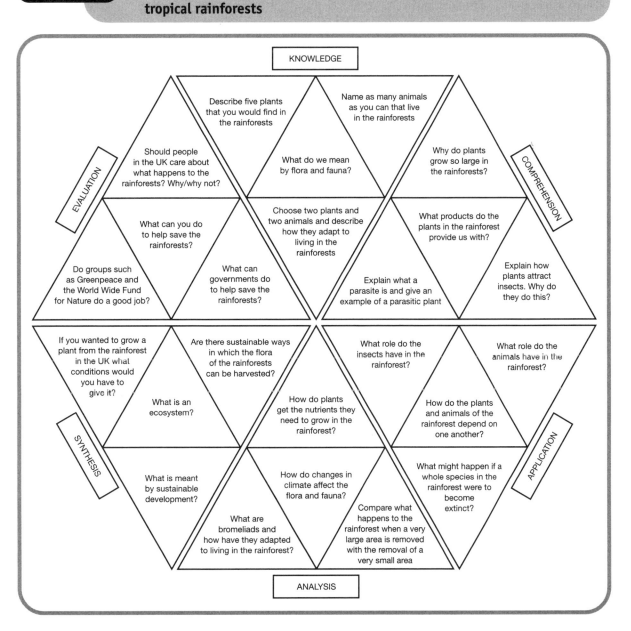

Diagram 5.6 **Thinking hexagon for studying the people and life of the tropical rainforests**

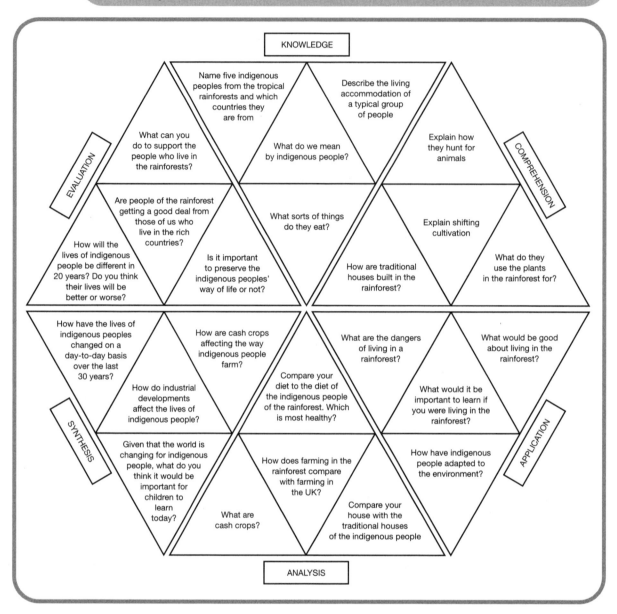

Groups should decide for themselves who will do what, however each pupil should do at least one collecting activity and one recording activity. Other activities may be negotiated with the help of the teacher.

Questions for the pupils to consider:

● Where will we find this information?

● How will we record it?

Step four: interpreting and evaluating

What does interpreting and evaluating involve for pupils?

1 Search for patterns and exceptions in results.

2 Select and use appropriate calculation skills.

3 Interpret any graphs and diagrams that were collected.

4 Check and evaluate any solutions.

5 Explain what the findings mean.

6 Explain the strengths and limitations of the evidence gathered.

7 Relate summarised data to the initial questions.

8 Suggest improvements to the methods used, where appropriate.

9 Suggest what more needs to be done in the field.

10 Identify and explain different views that people hold.

11 Appreciate the values and attitudes that people hold.

This can be achieved by the pupils:

- Sharing key findings (original groups are reformed and findings are shared).

- Forming new groups (i.e. pairs from the original groups join up to form new groups – each new group will have a variety of expertise).

- Making up analysis, synthesis and evaluation thinking triangles (Chapter 3) can help with interpretation and evaluation.

This stage of the project requires pupils to analyse evidence and to draw and justify conclusions. Each group must decide who will do what. Each pupil should do at least one interpreting and one evaluating task from the lists. Other activities may be negotiated with the teacher.

> **Questions for the pupils to consider:**
>
> - Can we now address the issue that we have chosen?
>
> - What can we say about it?

Step five: presenting data

What does presenting mean for pupils?

1 Drawing and producing (using paper and ICT) pie charts, diagrams, tables, line graphs, scatter graphs, frequency diagrams.

2 Using handwriting or ICT.

3   Writing, speaking or performing to inform, explain and describe.

4   Writing, speaking or performing to persuade, argue and advise.

5   Planning, drafting and redrafting.

6   Proofreading or editing.

7   Creating or compiling an object that represents an issue or key points.

It may culminate in a:

- written report;
- poster;
- radio programme;
- Powerpoint presentation to the class;
- game;
- poem;
- song;
- dance;
- play;
- video.

Everyone should be involved with the presentation of the information that has been collected. The pupils need to choose the best way of presenting the data to an audience and they need to feel comfortable with their choice. Once again each pupil should do at least one activity from the list. Other activities may be negotiated with the teacher.

The choice of presentation is based on the idea that it can be visual, auditory and/or kinaesthetic (as appropriate).

- **Visual** (poster, frieze, report etc).
- **Auditory** (presentation, song, music etc).
- **Kinaesthetic** (dance, game, drama, model, object etc).

Questions to consider

- How are our ideas best presented to other people?
- Who will do what?

Adding a second part to the project

So far so good! We have looked at ways of covering all five steps in the research process and certainly this will provide plenty of challenge for the majority of pupils. However, it is at this stage – when the pupils have gained a large amount of information and have processed this through analysis, synthesis and evaluation – that they are ready to deal with some larger and more complex issues. Most projects, unfortunately, do not go on to address these more complex issues.

If your class has carried out the project work outlined so far then there will be groups of pupils with expertise in various different areas related to the rainforests. If you remember the topics suggested were:

- location and climate;
- resources and industry;
- flora and fauna;
- people and ways of life.

Regrouping the pupils so that the new groups are formed which have representation from all the areas of expertise can mean that larger issues can be addressed, such as:

- conservation;
- global citizenship;
- international aid programmes;
- the role of interest groups such as Oxfam, Greenpeace etc.

Whole class project work, then, can be a two-part process where different steps can be emphasised and greater challenge can be assured (see Diagram 5.7).

- Part one involves grouping pupils according to existing expertise and interest to learn about a particular aspect of the topic.
- Part two involves regrouping the pupils into groups that are representative of all the areas studied to consider thematic questions about the topic.

Step one emphasises:

- the collection and recording of data;
- and the presentation of data.

Step two emphasises:

- the planning and the evaluation of the project;
- and the interpretation of data.

Diagram 5.7 **Whole class (two-part) project work**

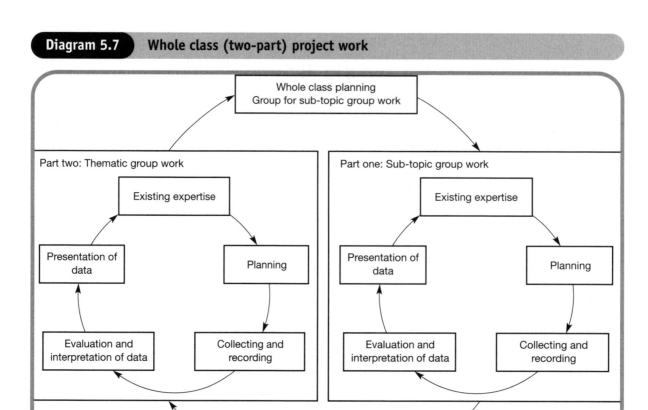

Diagram 5.8 **Thinking hexagon for conservation**

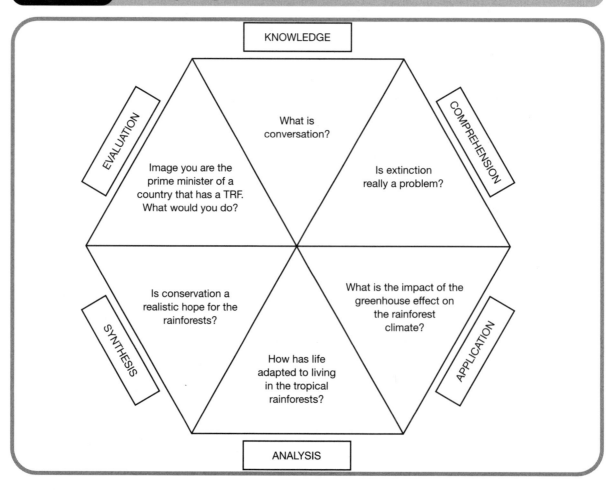

The Big Picture:
Part two

You now know a lot about the tropical rainforests. Your class has people who are experts in these topics:

- location and climate;

- resources and industry;

- flora and fauna;

- people and ways of life.

What you will be asked to do

- You are now going to be asked to use your expertise and work with people from other groups to think about one of these themes.
  - conservation;
  - global citizenship;
  - international aid;
  - the role of interest groups such as Oxfam, Greenpeace etc.

- You will decide with your teacher who will be in your group and which theme you should investigate. If you would rather you may negotiate with your teacher a different theme to investigate.

- You will be asked to go through the same five steps as before.
  - Step one: What do we already know?
  - Step two: What do we need to think about and plan?
  - Step three: How will we collect and record information?
  - Step four: What does all this tell us?
  - Step five: How will we decide what to tell others and how will we do this?

- Once you have gathered all the information you can about your theme your group will be asked to organise this information and then present it to the rest of the class.

Our group has decided to investigate _____

Members of our group are _____

_____

_____

_____

| Diagram 5.9 | Thinking hexagon for global citizenship |

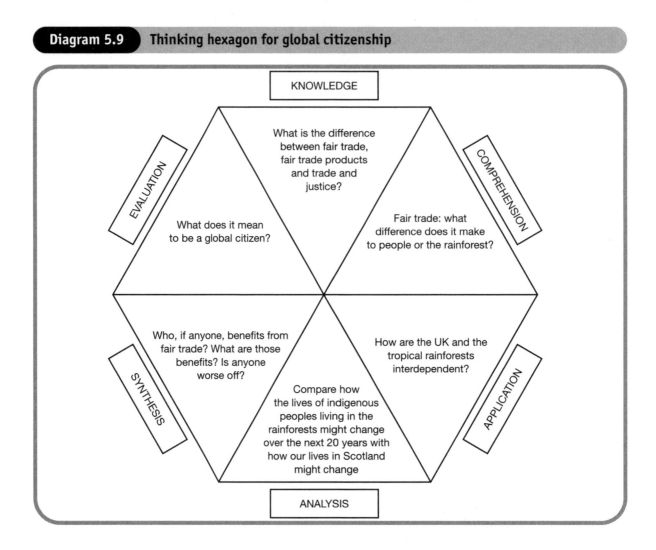

On page 79 you will find a photocopiable example of an advance organiser for part two of a project on tropical rainforests.

Class grouping for part two of the project

For part one of the project our class of 24 was grouped into four groups of six. For the second part of the project the groups should be reorganised so that new groups are formed (the number of groups will depend on the numbers in your class). Each new group should contain – where possible – a pair of experts from the original groups. (See Diagram 5.12.)

It is the second part of the process that allows the children to pool their expertise in order to tackle some of the more difficult issues. New information may have to be gathered but this can be organised when the groups are planning this new phase of the project. Each group should choose an issue to address. The suggestions on the advance organiser for part two of our project on tropical rainforests covered:

- conservation;

- the impact of the global economy on rainforest destruction;

Diagram 5.10 **Thinking hexagon for international aid**

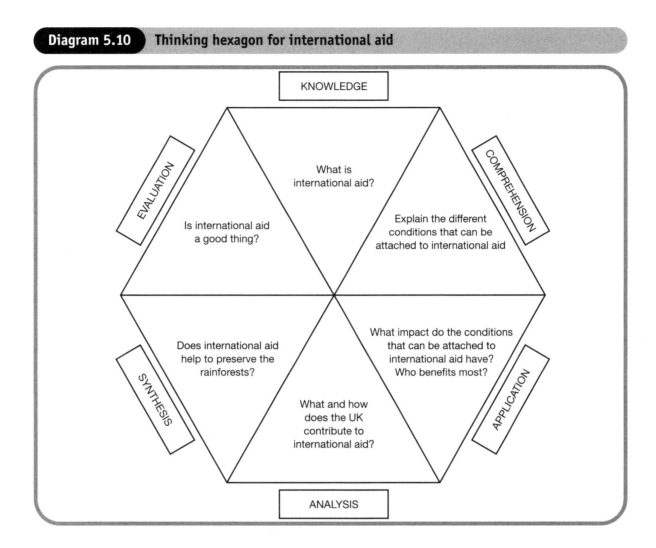

● global citizenship;

● international aid programmes.

The planning sheet from part one is easily used again for part two.

● Support and assessment

There are two further aspects of making project work suitable for whole classes that I want to cover before we finish. If we wish to raise the level of challenge in project work while still including everyone in the class then there are certain aspects of it that require particular attention. These are the things that make the difference between project work simply being an activity where children participate and it being a truly challenging and cognitively engaging learning experience for all. How we provide support and how we use assessment to support learning and to track the progress of individuals are crucial to the success of whole class projects.

Diagram 5.11 Thinking hexagon for the role of interest groups

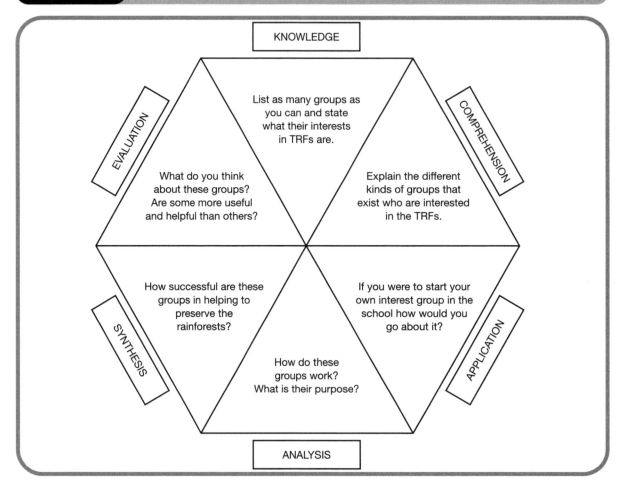

Diagram 5.12 Class grouping for the second part of the project

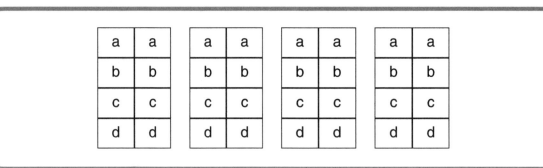

Providing support

Undertaking project work involves the use and development of certain skills. Pupils need to be able to:

● generate questions for investigation;

● collect and record data;

- interrogate text;

- access information;

- summarise and take notes;

- draft and redraft effectively;

- interpret information;

- use maps, diagrams and tables;

- analyse, synthesise and evaluate;

- go beyond the information they collect to see patterns, recommendations, consequences etc;

- generate different types of questions;

- prioritise information and activities.

These skills are important for all children to learn and develop but it is particularly true for gifted children. This is why project work is often identified as an ideal way of providing additional challenge in the curriculum. Within a class skill development will vary.

- Some pupils may already have these skills and need additional challenge in order to develop them.

- Some pupils may be developing these abilities and require practice in order to build confidence.

- Some pupils may require initial and explicit teaching of these skills.

As teachers we have to provide the appropriate support to them all. A tall order indeed!

In project work individualisation should come not in the form of different worksheets or activities but in the support and feedback that we give to different children. In an important piece of research in Scotland, feedback from the teacher was found to be the most sophisticated and effective form of differentiation that teachers can provide[iii]. There are various ways in which support can be offered in the classroom.

- feedback and support from the teacher;

- pupil grouping;

- peer support and mentoring;

- cross-age support and mentoring;

- home support;

- other adult support and mentoring;

- help sheets;

- the resources accessed;

- technology.

Project work is by its nature a collaborative affair and not something that should be undertaken individually. For gifted pupils it offers the opportunity of working with others who have different expertise and skills. If the class, as a whole, is not ready for an open ended activity then selecting a small group who are already demonstrating the appropriate prerequisite abilities may be more appropriate. The same two-part process will work for small groups as for whole class activities.

Alternatively, pupils can be grouped so that strengths are maximised and those not fully confident in some of the necessary skills can learn from others in the group. Decisions about how to group children can only be made by the class teacher. It is you who has the necessary depth of knowledge about the individuals in your class.

Using assessment to support pupils' work, provide feedback and track progress

We need to be able to keep track of the abilities that pupils are demonstrating. Formative assessment is often much more useful than summative and can be made in a variety of ways. I am going to suggest three things that might be assessed in this project by teachers and three forms of assessment that might be undertaken by pupils.

Teacher assessment

1 Assessing skill development. The skills related to each of the five steps of project work can be assessed on the basis of three stages of ability development:

- Developed ability:
  - demonstrated this ability independently of direction or support;
  - requires additional challenge.

- Emerging ability:
  - required direction but the ability began to emerge independently;
  - requires development and practice.

- New ability:
  - significant support required for ability to be demonstrated;
  - teaching, support and practice required.

Each skill can simply be rated D, E or N. Assessment sheets for skill development in each step (2–5) of the project have been provided. You will find these on pages 87–90.

2 Recording significant achievement[iv]. This means recording whatever the pupil has done particularly well. The pupils themselves can record this and it provides examples of particularly good work. Significant achievement may be recognised by the pupils themselves, their peers in their group or adults working with the children. Parents may be asked to contribute to this assessment process by recording any particularly good work carried out or demonstrated at home. A significant achievement can include a whole range of things such as:

- asking a really good question;

- coming up with an idea;

- chairing a group discussion; or

- helping others.

Significant achievement is very personal to the pupil. What might be significant for one pupil might not be so significant for another. A place to record significant achievement is provided in the assessment sheets for skill development in each step (2–5) of the project. You will find these sheets on pages 87–90.

3 Assessing the pupils' level of independence. Four levels of independence exist[v] and these have been used as a method of recording the level of independent learning that pupils display throughout the project.

- **Autonomous:** self-directed – the student autonomously creates the choice and self-evaluates the work.

- **Emerging autonomy:** self-directed to a degree – the student is involved in creating his/her own options within the teacher designed framework.

- **Reliant:** self-directed to a lesser degree – the teacher sets the work and the student chooses from a selection.

- **Dependent:** teacher-directed – the teacher sets the work and the pupil does it.

An assessment sheet to record independence for each of the steps (2–5) has been provided on page 91.

Pupil assessment

1   **Group assessment.** Having worked in groups the pupils might benefit from being given a chance to rate their own group's performance.

2   **Peer assessment.** This sheet asks pupils to identify the strengths displayed by peers. More than one name can be inserted for each of the questions posed.

3   **Self-assessment.** This sheet suggests a range of questions that pupils might use to reflect on their own work over the course of the project.

On pages 92–94 you will find sheets that will help you to record the different elements of assessment that have been suggested.

Points for reflection

- Project work needs to (and can) be more than a simple 'find out' exercise.

- There are five important steps to project work and pupils need to undertake them all in order to make the most of the learning opportunity.

- The grouping and regrouping of pupils for project work can raise the level of challenge for all.

- Thinking of project work in two parts can help to ensure that all the steps are covered.

Teacher Assessment
Skill Development
Planning Step

Assessment code

- **D**eveloped ability:
  - demonstrated this ability independently of direction or support;
  - requires additional challenge.

- **E**merging ability:
  - required direction but the ability began to emerge independently;
  - requires development and practice.

- **N**ew ability:
- significant support required for ability to be demonstrated;
- teaching, support and practice required.

Insert D, E or N in the appropriate box.

Cooperation with others
☐ Negotiated with others which aspect of the project to investigate as a group
☐ Worked with others to decide on a sequence of tasks
☐ Negotiated individual tasks within the group
☐ Participated in group discussions
☐ Contributed to the presentation of group plans to the whole class

Planning skills
☐ Identified possible areas for investigation
☐ Raised questions for investigation
☐ Justified choices of sources
☐ Justified choices of how to gather and record data

Decision-making and monitoring skills
☐ Decided on strategies, procedures sources and resources
☐ Justified choices
☐ Anticipated possible bias and suggested steps to counter
☐ Contributed to the completion of the group planning sheet
☐ Completed an individual planning sheet

Significant achievement

Teacher Assessment
Skill Development
Collecting and Recording Step

Assessment code

- **D**eveloped ability:
  - Demonstrated this ability independently of direction or support;
  - Requires additional challenge.

- **E**merging ability:
  - Required direction but the ability began to emerge independently;
  - Requires development and practice.

- **N**ew ability:
  - Significant support required for ability to be demonstrated;
  - Teaching, support and practice required.

Insert D, E or N in the appropriate box.

Collecting evidence

☐ A range of sources of evidence were considered and used
☐ Speaks with confidence to people
☐ Listens and responds to people appropriately
☐ Reads, listens and/or examines visually for information
☐ Identifies bias
☐ Uses checking procedures to confirm results
☐ Makes observations and measurements

Recording evidence

☐ Decided on recording devices
☐ Used note-taking
☐ Used ICT
☐ Used notation diagrams and symbols
☐ Used audio/video/ICT equipment

Significant achievement

Teacher Assessment
Skill Development
Interpreting and Evaluating

Assessment code

- **D**eveloped ability:
  - Demonstrated this ability independently of direction or support;
  - Requires additional challenge.

- **E**merging ability:
  - Required direction but the ability began to emerge independently;
  - Requires development and practice.

- **N**ew ability:
  - Significant support required for ability to be demonstrated;
  - Teaching, support and practice required.

Insert D, E or N in the appropriate box.

Interpreting

☐ Analysing evidence, drawing and justifying conclusions
☐ Searches for patterns and exceptions in results
☐ Selects and uses appropriate calculation skills
☐ Interprets a range of graphs and diagrams
☐ Checks and evaluates any solutions
☐ Explains what the findings show
☐ Explains the strengths and limitations of the evidence gathered
☐ Relates summarised data to the initial questions

Evaluating

☐ Suggests improvements to the methods used, where appropriate
☐ Suggests what more needs to be done in the field
☐ Identifies and explains different views that people hold
☐ Appreciates the values and attitudes that people hold

Significant achievement

Teacher Assessment
Skill Development
Presentation

Assessment code

- **D**eveloped ability:
  - Demonstrated this ability independently of direction or support;
  - Requires additional challenge.

- **E**merging ability:
  - Required direction but the ability began to emerge independently;
  - Requires development and practice.

- **N**ew ability:
  - Significant support required for ability to be demonstrated;
  - Teaching, support and practice required.

Insert D, E or N in the appropriate box.

Presenting

- ☐ Communicating in appropriate ways for the task and the audience
- ☐ Choosing the form and content to suit the purpose
- ☐ Choosing appropriate language and style
- ☐ Choosing the layout or format
- ☐ Drawing and producing (using paper and ICT) pie charts, diagrams, tables, line graphs, scatter graphs, frequency diagrams etc
- ☐ Using handwriting or ICT
- ☐ Writing or speaking to inform, explain and describe
- ☐ Writing or speaking to persuade, argue and advise
- ☐ Planning, drafting and redrafting
- ☐ Proofreading or editing

Significant achievement

Teacher Assessment of Independence

Record assessment by ticking the appropriate box

Name of pupil

Work undertaken during the planning step was

teacher initiated and directed	
from a framework provided by the teacher	
teacher led with the pupil offering suggestions	
pupil initiated and directed	

Work undertaken during the collecting and recording step was

teacher initiated and directed	
from a framework provided by the teacher	
teacher led with the pupil offering suggestions	
pupil initiated and directed	

Work undertaken during the interpreting and evaluating step was

teacher initiated and directed	
from a framework provided by the teacher	
teacher led with the pupil offering suggestions	
pupil initiated and directed	

Work undertaken during the presenting step was

teacher initiated and directed	
from a framework provided by the teacher	
teacher led with the pupil offering suggestions	
pupil initiated and directed	

Group Assessment

Circle the words that you think best describe the way your group worked

Rate your group's success in working cooperatively

Name of group

In negotiating activities we were:

     really good   good   not very good   poor

In organising the work we were:

     really good   good   not very good   poor

At making decisions we were:

     really good   good   not very good   poor

At giving ideas we were:

     really good   good   not very good   poor

At listening to others we were:

     really good   good   not very good   poor

At respecting others' views we were:

     really good   good   not very good   poor

At encouraging each other we were:

     really good   good   not very good   poor

In terms of everyone pulling their weight we were:

     really good   good   not very good   poor

We think our group did best at:

We think our group really needs to work at:

Peer Assessment

Put in the name of the people in your group who you think:

1   Knew a lot at the start.

2   Did really well at planning and organising.

3   Were really good at coming up with new ideas.

4   Did really well at collecting and recording information.

5   Were really good at organising information.

6   Were really good at presenting.

7   Were really good at seeing links between ideas and coming up with new ones.

8   Talked most.

9   Talked least.

10   Made most sense.

11   Were really good at organising other people.

12   Were really good at helping other people.

Self-Assessment

How did I find the work?

- What were the easiest bits?

- What were the hardest bits?

- What were the most enjoyable bits?

- What were the least enjoyable bits?

How do I feel about the five project steps?

- What do I feel confident about?

- What do I know and understand?

- What am I not so confident about?

- What would I like to learn to do better?

What did I think of

- The topic and theme that I studied?

- My own work?

- The work of others in the group?

How did I behave?

- Was I helpful to others?

- Was I patient with others?

- Was I polite and courteous to others?

- Did I concentrate well?

- Did I cover a lot of work?

Chapter 6

Conclusion

Over the years I have worked with a lot of different children, some of whom were identified as being gifted, some of whom were identified as having special educational needs and others who had no labels at all. They are all very clear about what it is that helps them to learn and they all identified the same sorts of things. These things are consistent with research into pupils' views of what makes a good teacher[i]. We could do worse than to aspire to what it is they tell us makes them a good learner and us a good teacher. So, let's leave the last words of this book to the children we teach and for whose benefit we read books such as this.

What helps me to become a good learner?

- If the topic is interesting.

- If I am learning new things, not just repeating what I can already do and already know.

- If I get a chance to have some say about what activities I do and how I do them.

- If my opinions and knowledge are valued.

- If I get a chance to show what I already know about the topic before we start.

- If the teacher asks me to help with preparing the topic.

- If I get to take chances and get things wrong.

- If I get the chance to learn from people in my class and at home and use this in my work.

- If I get the chance to sometimes work on my own and sometimes in groups. I like both ways of working.

- If I can work at my own pace and at things that are not too hard but also are not too easy.

This is more likely to happen if my teacher:

- Listens to what I have to say.

- Can be trusted to be fair, never to lose faith in me and treat me with respect.

- Learns from me as well as teaches me.

- Is relaxed and enjoys the day.

- Is able to laugh and have fun.

- Explains the work well and makes it interesting.

- Knows a lot about the topic and is enthusiastic and interested in it.

- Is flexible and can adjust things to suit individuals and circumstances.

- Reminds me of or helps to point out what it is I already know and have done before I start learning new things.

- Gives you a chance to make your own mistakes and learn from them.

- Always gives you the 'big picture' as well as the details.

- Expects that you can do well.

- Values and celebrates everyone's strengths in the class and supports those areas which need development.

- Talks to me at my level and gives me very clear and helpful feedback about my work.

- Organises for me to work with different groups of learners, sometimes these are others who have similar interests and sometimes it is others who are working at the same level.

- Provides activities that really challenge thinking and understanding.

A good teacher is one who:

- Doesn't humiliate you in front of the class; doesn't try to destroy you so that you'll leave school, or tell you that you're no good and that you should leave school.

- Doesn't write slabs of work on the board to be copied.

- Lets you talk and move about the classroom.

- Doesn't favour girls, or the boys who do what they're told.

- Doesn't keep picking on people who have a reputation, pushing them to retaliate.

- Doesn't mark you down because of your behaviour.

- Gives you a chance to muck up and learn from it.

Notes

Preface

i Some examples of those who suggest that implicit beliefs exists are Bruner (1996); Dweck (1999); Gibson (1984) and Sternberg (1990).

ii Sally Tomlinson (1982) in her seminal book entitled a *Sociology of Special Education* presented a powerful argument that categorisation and labelling of pupils with special educational needs was a socially constructed activity and was both deficit and individual in nature. Mary Poplin (1988) also suggested education was operating from a reductionist standpoint and that a new paradigm based on holism, structuralism and constructivism was required.

Chapter 1

i This idea comes from the work of Jerome Bruner (1996).

ii Three people who have undertaken research in this area are: Dweck (1999); Gibson (1984); and Sternberg (1990).

iii Sternberg (1990, p54).

iv Dweck (1999) called these theories 'entity' and 'incremental'. For the purposes of this book I have simplified this a little and simply called them 'fixed' and 'changeable'.

v Watson (1930, pp103).

vi There is a tendency in the work of people like Ames (1992) and Dweck (1999) to suggest that incremental theories are the correct theories for teachers to hold. This would have to be questioned as there is also evidence that performance goals and some aspects of an entity (fixed) theory of intelligence can be helpful.

vii This idea comes from Ames (1992).

viii This particular research was carried out by Dweck (1975).

ix A very good publication that outlines the main issues related to praise is *Is Praise Always a Good Thing?* SCCC (1996).

x This model was first devised by Smith and Docherty (1998) and appeared in a SNAP publication. It is used here with kind permission from SNAP and the authors.

xi This idea came from the work of Freeman (1998).

xii This idea came from the work of Kennard (1998).

xiii This list is adapted from the work of Costa (accessed online 2004).

Chapter 2

i From an article by Kearney (1996) which was accessed online.

ii Passow (1988), for example, expressed concern about the narrow range of provision that is in place for gifted students.

iii Passow (1988) p80.

iv Tannenbaum (1983) p423 in a similar vein to Passow.

v These four elements of learning are suggested by Jerome Bruner (1996).

Chapter 3

i   This idea of stages of dependence comes from Treffinger (1975).

ii   If you want to read more about Bloom's taxonomy the sources of his ideas were published in Bloom *et al* (1964).

iii This theory was published in one of Howard Gardner's early books (Gardner, 1983). The major problem with using Gardner's theory for the purposes of framing such activities is that they were not designed to be used in this way. While they offer a framework to expand the range of activities on offer they do not provide a hierarchical approach. There is no discernable difference in levels of difficulty between the activities. This is not to say that using this theory has no practical application and can be helpful when trying to ensure variety in designing tasks.

iv   Gardner (1999) p28.

v   Gardner (1999) p28.

vi   Gardner (1999) p45.

vii Gardner (1999) p66.

viii You can read more about Osborn's work in Osborn (1957).

ix   This idea comes from a book by Joan Dalton (1985).

x   You can read about reciprocal teaching in an article by Palinscar and Brown (1984).

Chapter 5

i   Painter, J. (1996) Article accessed online 25.2.04. http://www.nexus.edu.au/teachstud/gat/painter.htm

ii   The artefact was a schoolbag with contents. This represented many of the issues that the candidate had studied on her course.

iii This research was carried out by Simpson *et al* (1989).

iv   This phrase comes from a series of books called Tracking Significant Achievement. You will find these books by Clarke and Atkinson (1996), Glauert (1996) and Sainsbury (1996) listed in the bibliography.

v   This idea comes from Treffinger (1975).

Conclusion

i   For a really good piece of research into what boys think of schools and teachers see Slade and Trent (2000). Some of the ideas children expressed in this research have been incorporated here.

Bibliography

Ames, C. (1992) Classrooms: goals, structures and student motivation. *Journal of Educational Psychology*. 84 (3), pp261–271.

Bloom, B. J., Krathowhl, D. R. and Masia, B. B. (1964) *Taxonomy of Educational Objectives: The classification of educational goals*. Longman: New York.

Bruner, J. (1996) *The Culture of Education*. Cambridge, MA: Harvard University Press.

Clarke, S. and Atkinson, S. (1996) *Tracking Significant Achievement in Primary Mathematics*. Hodder and Stoughton: Bath.

Costa, A. What human beings do when they behave intelligently and how they can become more so. http://www.eddept.wa.edu.au/gifttal/EAGER/Arthur%20L%20Costa.html (accessed online 1 Dec 2004).

Dalton, J. (1985) *Adventures in Thinking: Creative Thinking and Co-operative Talk in Small Groups*. Nelson: Melbourne.

Dweck, C. S. (1975) The role of expectations and attributions in the alleviation of learned helplessness. *Journal of Personality and Social Psychology*, 31, pp674–685.

Dweck, C. S. (1999) *Self Theories: Their Role in Motivation, Personality and Development*. Philadelphia: Psychology Press.

Freeman, J. (1998) *Educating the Very Able: Current International Research*. London: The Stationery Office.

Gardner, H. (1983) *Frames of Mind: The Theory of Multiple Intelligences*. New York: Basic Books.

Gardner, H. (1999) *Intelligence Reframed*. Basic Books: New York.

Gibson, R. (1984) *Structuralism and Education*. London: Hodder and Stoughton.

Glauert, E. (1996) *Tracking Significant Achievement in Primary Science*. Hodder and Stoughton: Bath.

Kearney, K. (1996) Highly gifted children in full inclusion classrooms. Accessed online http://www.hollingworth.org/fullincl.html 1 Dec 2004. This article first appeared in *Highly Gifted Children*, Summer/Fall 1996, 12 (4).

Kennard, R. (1998) Providing for mathematically able children in ordinary classrooms. *Gifted Education International*. Vol 13 pp28–35.

Osborn, Alex, F. (1957) *Applied Imagination: Principles and procedures of creative problem solving*. New York: Scribner.

Painter, J. (1996) Questioning techniques for gifted students. Accessed online 25.2.04 http://www.nexus.edu.au/teachstud/gat/painter.htm

Palinscar, A. S. and Brown, A. L. (1984) Reciprocal teaching of comprehension fostering and comprehension monitoring activities *Cognition and Instruction* 1. 117–175.

Passow, A. H. (1988) Reflections on three decades of education of the gifted. *Gifted Education International* V5, N2.

Poplin, M. (1988) Holistic/constructivist principles of the teaching/learning process. Implications for the field of learning disabilities, *Journal of Learning Disabilities*, 21 (7): 401–16.

Sainsbury, M. (1996) *Tracking Significant Achievement in Primary English*. Hodder and Stoughton: Bath.

Scottish Consultative Council on the Curriculum (SCCC) (1996) *Is Praise Always a Good Thing?* SCCC: Dundee.

Simpson, M., Cameron, P., Goulder, J., Duncan, A. and Smithers, I. (1989) *Differentiation in the Primary School: Investigations of learning and teaching*. Northern College: Aberdeen.

Slade, M. and Trent, F. (2000) What the boys are saying: An examination of the views of boys about declining rates of achievement and retention. *International Education Journal* V1, N3, pp201–229.

Smith, C. M. M. and Doherty, M. (1998) *Identifying Abilities in Individual Curricular Areas*. The Scottish Network for Able Pupils (SNAP): St Andrews College of Education, Glasgow.

Sternberg, R. J. (1990) *Metaphors of the Mind: Conceptions of the Nature of Intelligence*. Cambridge: Cambridge University Press.

Tannenbaum, A. J. (1983) *Gifted Children: Psychological and educational perspectives*. Macmillan: New York.

Tomlinson, S. (1982) *The Sociology of Special Education*. London: Routledge.

Treffinger, D. J. (1975) Teaching for self-directed learning: A priority for the gifted and talented. *Gifted Children Quarterly* 19 46–59.

Watson, J. B. (1930) *Behaviourism* (rev ed.) University of Chicago Press: Chicago.

Glossary

Cognitive engagement Where learners are interacting with the topic, course or programme in a way that changes their thinking.

Divergent questioning Questions that encourage people to think 'outside the box'. Divergent questions encourage creativity by linking ideas to normally unrelated ideas.

Entity theory of intelligence A theory which holds that intelligence is general, fixed and innate.

Formative assessment Final and formal assessment that occurs at the end of a piece of work, course or programme.

Incremental theory of intelligence A theory which holds that intelligence is multi-variant, flexible and environmentally determined.

Indigenous people People who are native or local to the area.

Intrapersonal intelligence The ability to know and understand oneself.

Mastery orientated learning Where the learner is primarily concerned with the process of learning. In other words the desire to understand outweighs the desire to get things right.

Performance orientated learning Where the learner is primarily concerned with the products of learning. In other words the desire to get the right answer or be the best in the class outweighs the desire to understand the process.

Quescussion A discussion that only uses questions. No statements are allowed.

Reciprocal teaching All individuals in the group take on the role of teacher. Learners learn by teaching one another.

Summative assessment Assessment that is usually informal, is ongoing and which builds an overall picture from a variety of sources and settings.

Taxonomy A hierarchical classification of skills. Benjamin Bloom suggested that there was a set of six thinking skills that could be classified hierarchically. The lower order skills (in ascending order) include: knowledge, comprehension and application. The higher order skills (in ascending order) include: analysis, synthesis and evaluation.

Theory of multiple intelligences A theory put forward by Howard Gardner which suggests that we all have at least seven separate and distinct intelligences rather than a single general intelligence.

Index